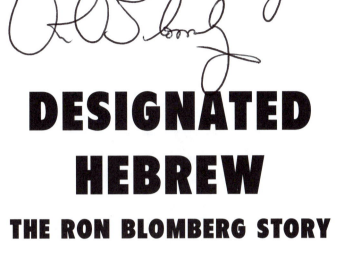

DESIGNATED HEBREW

HEBREW

THE RON BLOMBERG STORY

Ron Blomberg
and Dan Schlossberg

SportsPublishingLLC.com

Publishers: Peter L. Bannon and Joseph J. Bannon Sr.
Senior managing editor: Susan M. Moyer
Acquisitions editor: Mike Pearson
Developmental editor: Doug Hoepker
Art director: K. Jeffrey Higgerson
Dust jacket design: Dustin J. Hubbart
Interior layout: Dustin J. Hubbart and Heidi Norsen
Imaging: Dustin J. Hubbart and Kenneth J. O'Brien
Photo editor: Erin Linden-Levy

Printed in the United States of America

Sports Publishing L.L.C.
804 North Neil Street
Champaign, IL 61820

Phone: 1-877-424-2665
Fax: 217-363-2073
www.SportsPublishingLLC.com

Library of Congress Cataloging-in-Publication Data

Blomberg, Ron, 1948-
   Designated Hebrew : the Ron Blomberg story / Ron Blomberg, with Dan Schlossberg ; foreword by Marty Appel.
      p. cm.
   ISBN 1-58261-987-5 (alk. paper)
   1. Blomberg, Ron, 1948- 2. Jewish baseball players—United States—Biography. 3. Baseball players—United States—Biography. 4. New York Yankees (Baseball team) I. Schlossberg, Dan, 1948- II. Title.

GV865.B555A3 2006
796.357092—dc22

                         2006002782

For Beth, Adam, and Chesley

CONTENTS

FOREWORD

BY MARTY APPEL

irst off, after all these years, what's with the "Bloom-berg" pronunciation? If it's "*Blooom-berg,*" how come his first name isn't pronounced "Roon?" Just wanted to get that out of the way.

My friend Ron Blomberg has always been just a little off-center, enough to confuse and confound. And to make you smile. Our Yankee careers paralleled each other's (although I'd have traded every day of mine in the front office to have played one game, and to have my name in the *Baseball Encyclopedia*). He was the nation's first selection in the June 1967 free agent draft, and his selection by the struggling Yankees was a huge national story. He was to be the "Great Jewish Hope," the big box-office attraction, the wondrous slugger of long Yankee Stadium home runs. He had the body, the appetite, and the innocence of the cartoon character L'il Abner, although I'm not sure younger readers will know who that is. (For the uninformed, go to www.lil-abner.com)

Quietly, that same summer, I was interviewing in the team's front office for a summer job in the public relations department, answering Mickey Mantle's fan mail. By 1970 I was the assistant PR Director, and Ronnie was with us in spring training in Ft. Lauderdale, charming the New York media with the great smile, the southern charm, the innocent observations, and the remarkable power to take a fastball from a right-handed pitcher and propel it great distances.

The "Blomberg Watch" began around that time, everyone hoping that he would bring that great bat to New York ASAP and help the depressed franchise. No one wanted it more than the CBS executives running the club, struggling to draw a million fans a year. He joined the team in the summer of '71, on the same day the Yanks acquired another Ron—Swoboda—and put two instant media delights in uniform at once. One Ron was on the way up, the other on the way down, but for a time, the news cameras would head for Yankee Stadium for some good stories. In that first week, Dick Schapp, doing local sports for WNBC-TV, asked me to bring Ron to the set for a live interview. He knew a good story.

"C'mon, Bloomie," I said, "We're going to go on Channel 4 with Dick Schaap!"

He had trouble with the name. He kept repeating it as we drove downtown. "Jack Snapp, Jack Snapp, Jack Snapp."

"No, no, no," I said, "it's Dick Schaap! He's pretty famous, you know!"

"Got it," he said.

"Jack Snapp, Jack Snapp, Jack Snapp."

I sighed.

He was on the set, *Live at Five*.

"…and now we've got the Yankees' new first baseman, Ron Blomberg, with us," said Schaap, "and Boomer, thanks for joining us."

"Nice to be with you … Dick."

Not only did he nail it, but on live TV he turned towards me off in the wings and winked. He was impossibly funny.

We became neighbors in Riverdale, a nice section of the Bronx about 12 minutes from Yankee Stadium, and we socialized a lot. Furious games of table ice hockey—the game where you control the players by pulling levers in and out—turned into a league with standings. His neighbor, Dr. Stanley Gedzelman, a noted meteorologist on the staff of City College, was dragged into the competition. Bloomie usually won.

He ate prodigiously, but needed the comfort of the familiar. He hated to try new places or new foods. Once he settled into a place, he liked returning over and over, and always asked for a full pitcher of water on the table. When the social occasion seemed to call for the maturity of ordering a mixed drink, he would order a vodka gimlet—he must have heard someone else doing it—but would never take a sip.

I went to Atlanta with him and his first wife, Mara (I'm still friends with her, too), during the World Series of 1973. He had little interest in watching the Mets-Oakland games. He was not a spectator, and his attention span was fairly limited. I once gave Mara something for their home and she said, "This would go well in Ronnie's study," which I thought was a fantastic oxymoron, until I realized she was serious.

We stayed at his parents' home, and his mother, Goldie, was constantly reminding him to towel off the sink in the bathroom, because he had a habit of splashing the room full of water. I thought I was having a sleepover at a fifth grader's home. In his driveway, we played home run derby with wiffle balls and a plastic bat. The road was a home run. I reached it a few times—imagine being proud of hitting a wiffle ball home run 75 feet off a major league first baseman—but what I really remember is him hitting a line drive off me, or rather through me. I think the ball entered my chest cavity, came out the back, and still reached the road.

Oh, could he hit. You had to be there in Yankee Stadium to see the batting practice shots he sent into orbit because, of course, they didn't make the box scores or game stories. I believe—I'm too much a perfectionist when it comes to history to say I'm sure—that he hit the famous old Yankee Stadium façade once or twice during batting practice, the place where Mantle had twice done it, quite famously, in regular-season games.

We went to Cooperstown together for a winter sports banquet some time after his "first DH bat" was put on display, and he posed with his bat and asked the director of the Hall of Fame, poor old Kenny Smith, the most outrageous question about local village customs that had surely ever been asked by a visitor to that innocent little town. I'm not sure that Kenny ever recovered.

Bloomie was an usher at my wedding and walked my 75-year-old grandmother down the aisle, totally enjoying the attention and his mission.

I never saw anyone better with fans. He signed, he posed, he *kibitzed*, he learned their names, and if he was too busy, he'd politely make up some outrageous excuse about why he couldn't stop at that moment. ("I've got to go study to be a doctor and a lawyer like my parents wanted.")

He went to dinner with sportswriters, one of the few players to do that. They were just as good company as his teammates as far as he was concerned. The only real criteria he had for dinner was that the helpings be plentiful and it not last more than an hour. The attention-span thing.

As for his career, he certainly had some highlights—hitting .400 as late as the 4th of July one year to share a *Sports Illustrated* cover, and of course, the first DH thing, in which I played a small role by getting the bat up to Cooperstown (only bat in Cooperstown that celebrates a walk!)—but mostly, and sadly, his was another career that failed to reach its potential. He was riddled with injuries, including the one that essentially ended his career, crashing into the wall in Winter Haven, Florida, running down an unimportant spring training drive while playing in unfamiliar left field. Defense was not his strong suit, either at first or the outfield, but that was pretty much the end of the Blomberg era in New York. He was technically a member of the championship teams of 1976 and 1977, but he played one game in those two years. I called him at home to get him in the team photo because I figured someday he'd want to show his son, Adam, that he was on a pennant-winning team.

The Yankees weren't happy when he opted for free agency and went to the White Sox in '77. They had paid for his rehab, and now he was bolting. But he needed a fresh start. He loved the Yankees, but the team had really passed him by; he wasn't a favorite of Billy Martin's, and he needed to make a name for himself somewhere else. Sadly, it didn't happen for him in Chicago, either, and that was the end of his short but fabled career.

We've kept in touch like two old pals, and the fact that he is a former big leaguer has become largely irrelevant, except when he's called to ask me about the growing value of his "first DH" status in baseball history. I know he could still put a wiffle ball through my chest, and he knows that I can name all the MVPs from the beginning of time, but geez, we're both going to turn 60 one of these days, and it's nice to have a friend who makes you still feel like a kid.

The attention span, however, is still a little lacking.

"Hey big guy, how ya' doing," he'll say, when he initiates a phone call. And then after a minute or two, comes, "Listen big guy, ya gonna be home later? Let me give you a call!" He was the one who made the call in the first place. He's impossible. And this is why I love him.

Marty Appel
New York, NY

Marty Appel was in the Yankees public relations department, including four years as director, from 1968-77, and followed that by serving as executive producer of the team's telecasts. He is the author of 16 books, including Thurman Munson's autobiography, and his own memoir, Now Pitching *for the Yankees. He operates Marty Appel Public Relations in New York City.*

INTRODUCTION

BY DAN SCHLOSSBERG

When young Ron Blomberg told his friends he wanted to play major-league baseball, they practically laughed him out of town. With the exception of a rare superstar like Sandy Koufax, Jewish kids just didn't do that. Most came from backgrounds that emphasized education, with resulting careers as doctors or lawyers. Blomberg's parents were different: they let their only child ride his athletic skills as far as possible. And they probably realized, too, that Ron lacked the discipline to be a doctor.

Baseball requires a discipline of its own. Getting to the majors wasn't easy even *without* the handicap of religious prejudice. Hank Greenberg, who endured a lot of it during the Thirties, once said, "Every time I hit a home run, I feel like I'm striking a blow against Hitler." Greenberg was playing first base for Pittsburgh in 1947 when Jackie Robinson, baseball's first black player, reached base. The veteran slugger told the rookie, "I know what you're going through. I'll help you get through it." Without that support, the game's history—and the country's—might be remarkably different.

Ethnic tensions in the big leagues remained high even after Robinson broke the baseball color line. Many teams were slow to sign their own black players—the Red Sox were the last in 1969—or promote other minorities. The only Jewish presence in the majors from 1982-88 was a forgettable seven-game stint for Mark Gilbert. Near the end of the 2005 season, a player asked a team chaplain whether Jews were "doomed" because they didn't believe in Jesus. That shouldn't have happened in an era with a record number of Jewish players in the majors.

Ron Blomberg was a trailblazer: in addition to being the first designated hitter—an accident of fate—he was also the first significant Jewish Yankee. The Brooklyn Dodgers and New York Giants thought Jewish players would widen their fan base, but the Yankees had no apparent interest. The only *lantzman* who preceded Blomberg to the Bronx hid behind the pseudonym of Jimmie Reese.

Blomberg didn't believe in hiding: he loved people almost as much as he loved to eat. He even went out to eat with the writers, a habit completely foreign to most major leaguers. As long as a good corned beef sandwich was part of the deal, he was there. Unfortunately for Blomberg, corned beef couldn't do for him what spinach did for Popeye. He had great hand-eye coordination, a powerful lefthanded stroke, and a willingness to work hard, but he couldn't avoid the injury bug. Once billed as "the next Mickey Mantle," he managed only 52 career home runs, though six were against future Hall of Famers and two more came against Cy Young Award winners who didn't reach Cooperstown.

He still accomplished a lot, however, and was present for plenty of note. The Boomer was there when George Steinbrenner arrived, when Billy Martin became Yankee manager, when the team traded superstars with San Francisco, and when two Yankee pitchers traded families. He watched the Yankees battle themselves as well as their opponents, winning their first pennant in 12 years in 1976 and their first World Series in 15 years the following season.

A witness to cross burnings and synagogue bombings in his youth, Blomberg felt relieved when New York's large Jewish population embraced him. He felt even more at home after the team landed fellow Jews Elliott Maddox and Ken Holtzman during his tenure in the Bronx. Still maintaining his ties to the game, Blomberg joined Maddox and Holtzman in a 2004 Cooperstown program honoring Jewish major leaguers. Norm Sherry, Richie Scheinblum, Mike Epstein, and Bob Tufts also participated, along with Martin Abramowitz, creator of the Jewish Major Leaguers card set for the American Jewish Historical Society (AJHS). For Blomberg, as well as the throng of media and fans who attended, the Jewish weekend was a joy. They traded autographs and anecdotes, conducted a hitting clinic for kids, and chowed down on the first Kosher meals ever served at the Baseball Hall of Fame.

That weekend, Holtzman recalled when he was asked to pitch batting practice between starts because the Cubs were scheduled to face Koufax, who also threw lefthanded, in the game that night. Cub hitters fared poorly, prompting Holtzman to tell coach Lou Klein, "If they can't hit me, they sure aren't going to hit *him*." That was the night Koufax pitched the only perfect game of his career.

A year earlier, Koufax had opted out of pitching the 1965 World Series opener because of a conflict with Rosh Hashanah, the Jewish New Year. Don Drysdale worked in his stead and got bombed. When Dodger manager Walter Alston came out to relieve him, Drysdale said, "I bet you wish I were Jewish, too."

Koufax roomed with Norm Sherry, a second-string catcher whose coaching tips turned the once-wild lefthander into a Hall of Famer. The pair also enjoyed Jewish food and were delighted to find bagels and lox on a room service menu in Pittsburgh. They tried to eat it but found it too salty. "Don't worry, Sandy," Sherry said, "my brother will eat anything." Called to the room, Larry Sherry quickly proved his brother right by devouring the platter.

Attendees of the Cooperstown conference, including Blomberg, devoured the stories. They heard about Moses Solomon, called "the Rabbi of Swat" after a 49-homer season in Class C, and Moe Berg, a World War II spy who could speak 11 languages but couldn't hit a curveball. Neither made it big in the big leagues.

Most Jews don't. That's why they are writers, broadcasters, and public relations directors—including seven different ones with the Yankees alone during the George Steinbrenner regime that started in 1973. The first of those seven was Marty Appel, who became so close to Blomberg that the player served as an usher at Appel's wedding. Now a highly respected New York sports publicist, Marty also helped organize the Jewish baseball weekend in Cooperstown.

I'm glad Ron Blomberg was there. It would have been a shame for the first DH—Designated Hebrew—to have not been in attendance.

THE FIRST DH

will never forget what happened on April 6, 1973. That's when I became a part of baseball history as the first designated hitter. The circumstances were accidental: our game against the Red Sox started earlier in the day than any other game, and so we had first crack at the record book. My team, the Yankees, batted first because we were the visiting team, and I got to bat in the first inning—thus making me the first designated hitter.

By all rights, Boston's Orlando Cepeda should have been the first DH; he batted fifth in the Red Sox batting order, and I was hitting sixth for the Yankees. If we would have gone down with a whimper in the top of the first, and the Red Sox could have had a couple guys reach base in the bottom of the first, that honor would belong to Cepeda. He was acquired by the Red Sox that off-season to be Boston's full-time DH just one week after the American League adopted the designated-hitter rule. I was an accidental DH, just as Gerald Ford would become an accidental president a year later. But history smiled on me that day, as my teammates loaded the bases with two outs in the top of the first, bringing me to the plate for a historic at-bat.

I wasn't so aware of its significance at the time, however. The DH was new to baseball in 1973, and it took me by surprise, too. I knew DH meant "designated hitter," but I didn't really understand just what sort of role the designated hitter was supposed to play. Nor did I think the DH would have any impact on my career.

It was a rule born from ownership greed. Offense in the American League was down, and the owners thought they could boost attendance by replacing the pitcher's slot in the lineup with a professional hitter. The owners felt the change would increase scoring and keep fans more interested in the game. Following suit with ownership's train of thought, most teams selected sluggers to fill the DH spot, replacing the weakest hitter in the order with one of the strongest hitters on the team.

When I first heard about the new rule, I thought it was a big joke. It didn't surprise me that A's owner Charley Finley was one of its big backers. Known as a micromanager who would try anything to raise fan interest, Finley had tried a laundry list of stunts, like introducing brightly colored uniforms and orange baseballs; pushing for World Series night games; making a live mule the team mascot; introducing a mechanical rabbit that would pop up behind home plate to give the umpire new baseballs; encouraging his players to grow facial hair; and shortening the distance from home plate to right field by expanding his bleachers into something he called his "pennant porch." Finley thought that duplicating the short right field of Yankee Stadium would provide similar success for his team. He was wrong about that gimmick, but he was right about the DH. He even got Bowie Kuhn, the commissioner of baseball at the time, to agree with him, which didn't happen often. (Kuhn later rejected Finley's plea for a "designated runner.")

The rule was originally called the "DPH," which stood for designated pinch-hitter. Kuhn cast the deciding vote when the two leagues deadlocked on the issue of adopting the rule. The American League strongly endorsed it, but the National League was just as adamant in its opposition. The commissioner couldn't get the leagues to agree, so he decided to allow the A.L. to try it on an experimental basis. Even though it had been tried earlier in the minors, nobody thought it was going to last longer than the allotted length of the experiment: three years.

I didn't think much about the DH at the time. I recall during spring training in 1973 watching Ralph Houk, our manager, hang up the Yankee lineup card. I was used to seeing the pitcher hit. So was our best pitcher, Mel Stottlemyre, who was also a pretty good hitter…for a pitcher. But under the DH rule, Mel wasn't going to get that chance, despite having seven career home runs. The times were changing.

During spring training that year, I didn't make a single appearance as a DH. That role was reserved for Felipe Alou or Johnny Callison. I played in the outfield and at first base and hit against a lot of left-handed pitchers—something that didn't happen too often in my career since I batted left-handed. I was crushing the ball in exhibition games, so my playing time was plentiful. A week before spring training ended, I ran out a ball and pulled a hamstring while stretching to reach the first-base bag. The injury was treated as usual, and I figured I'd be ready to play when the season started. When we broke camp, however, my hamstring was still bothering me a little bit. I was swinging the bat pretty well, but my leg was still taped up.

As we caught our flight to Boston for Opening Day, I asked Marty Appel, our publicity director, who was going to pitch for the Red Sox. If it was a lefty, I knew I might be benched; but if it was a right-hander, I was sure to get the nod. When I found out righty Luis Tiant was scheduled to pitch, I was happy. I knew I'd be in the lineup.

On the plane, Elston Howard told me that Houk wanted to have a word with me. That's not the sort of thing a player wants to hear as the team departs from spring training. I assumed my roster spot was safe because I had been hitting so well. Plus the Yankees had released some players to make room for me on the roster.

I was relieved—and a little dumbfounded—when Ralph asked me, "What do you think about being the DH?"

"Skipper, I really don't know too much about it," I replied. "What do I have to do?"

"You get up to bat, you take your four swings, you drive in runs, you come back to the bench, and you keep loose in the runway," Houk told me. "You're basically pinch-hitting for the pitcher four times in the same game.

"I can't play you in the field because your leg is so bad, but at least this will give us an opportunity to get your bat into the lineup."

That sounded great to me. If Ralph thought I could help the team the most by being the DH, it was fine with me. I loved to play in the field, but I also knew I was more valuable to the club at the plate than in the field. When we arrived in Boston the papers printed the probable lineups for opening day, and there I was hitting sixth for the Yankees.

When I arrived at Fenway Park the following day it was freezing outside. In previous seasons, when we had opened the season in New York or at Cleveland or Detroit, and the weather was miserable, the players would call the writers who served as scorekeepers in the pressbox and say, jokingly, "I'll take my 0-for-4 already so I don't have to play." Transitioning from 90-degree weather in Florida to 35-degree weather up north was tough.

As Ray Fitzgerald wrote about Opening Day at Fenway in 1973 for *The Boston Globe:* "The game didn't need a designated hitter. It needed a designated meteorologist." It was cold and windy, just a dismal day. I was the type of athlete who had to run and stretch his legs in order to work up a good sweat before I played. I was born and raised in Atlanta, Georgia, so I was never fond of cold weather. But this weather was just offensive. Bobby Murcer had his hands wrapped around a hot-water bottle, and most of my teammates were wearing gloves and knit hats during batting practice.

I took batting practice before the game as usual and then grabbed my glove and trotted out to first base to shag some balls. Ellie Howard shouted toward me, "You're not playing first base today. I don't want you to hurt your hamstring anymore. Come back to the cage and keep hitting." Everybody liked to hit, but hitting in that cold weather made my hands sting. I wasn't thrilled with the extra batting practice, but it served to settle my nerves. I was anxious to see how I would perform in my new role of designated hitter.

As game time approached, the Fenway Park public address announcer, Sherm Feller, introduced both teams. After the National Anthem was performed, I couldn't sit still, so I ran up and down the runway track between the dugout and the clubhouse to stay warm. Several of my teammates were in the clubhouse trying to keep warm. Trying to work up a sweat, I did a few sit-ups.

Meanwhile, my team was busy heating up the basepaths. With two outs, Matty Alou doubled to center. Murcer and Graig Nettles followed with walks, which brought me to the plate with a chance to give the fans their first look at a DH in action. Tiant was throwing a lot of junk that day, trying to confuse the hitters with his deceptive windup. I asked Carlton Fisk, who was catching that day for the Sox, what Tiant was throwing. "He's throwing it right by you," Fisk told me. But Tiant couldn't find the plate. Just as the previous two batters had done, I worked him for a walk, driving in the first run of the game. We then scored two more when Felipe Alou doubled to right.

When the inning ended, I was waiting for somebody to run out there and throw me my glove. Dick Howser, our third-base coach, told me to come sit next to him on the bench. I was so used to playing in the field that I had forgotten that as the designated hitter I was going to spend a lot of time on the bench. So I plopped down next to Howser, who told me, "Why don't you go into the clubhouse and tell the clubhouse guy to make you some food?" He was a man after my heart, since I loved to eat. But considering that I was also freezing to death, his idea was genius. Our clubhouse attendant, Vince Orlando, had the radio on in the locker room so I could listen to the game while enjoying some hot chocolate.

I finished the game 1-for-3, but we lost, 15-5, as the Red Sox pummeled us for 20 hits. Stottlemyre got knocked out early and Fisk hit two home runs, including a grand slam. But Boston's DH, Cepeda, wore the collar at 0-for-6. I went into the clubhouse, where guys were hanging around as usual enjoying cold cuts from the postgame spread, and was surprised to find 35 or 40 reporters waiting for me at my locker. That was the first time I sensed that I was part of history. Up until then, the significance of being Major League Baseball's first DH was totally lost on me.

Marty Appel ran up to me and demanded that I turn over my bat. I protested: "Marty, I can't give you my bat because this bat has good wood in it. This is my bat." But Marty was persuasive. "We're sending it up to Cooperstown, to the Hall of Fame," he said. Photographers snapped photos of me, and I added my No. 12 jersey to the pile of memorabilia Marty was sending off to Cooperstown. At dinner later that night, Marty asked me what it was like to be the first DH. I shrugged, laughing off the honor. I still thought it was a joke and that the rule was never going to last.

I was the designated hitter again the following day, and then switched back and forth between DH and first base over the next few games before settling back in as the regular first baseman during May. I was crushing the ball, hitting hard line drives and majestic home runs. My average climbed to over .400 in June, but Houk still wouldn't let me hit against lefties. All the sportswriters questioned his judgment, asking why I wasn't starting against lefties despite my success against right-ies. I had never hit too well against lefthanders during the previous two seasons, so Houk probably felt there wasn't much of a chance that I would improve despite my hot hitting.

Reporters hounded me for a quote, practically begging me to say something critical of the manager for not playing me against left-handed pitchers. But I didn't want any controversy. I was not the type of person who wanted to cause a stir. I knew that once I caused friction in the clubhouse, it would only get worse—especially if I went into a slump. So I kept my mouth shut. After all, we were winning—by late June the Yankees were 10 games over .500 and leading the A.L. East—and I was hitting so well I didn't want to do anything to jinx our good luck. Others were taking note of our success, too. I wound up on the covers of *Sports Illustrated* and *The Sporting News* as the season wore on, and I was even asked to appear on telethons.

Murcer and I were the Yankee glamour boys. *Sports Illustrated* called us the "pride of the new Yankees" on their cover, and wrote in their article that Murcer, Thurman Munson, and I gave the Yankees the nucleus for a great team. I started receiving calls from agents who wanted to represent me in negotiations with companies who wanted me to appear in commercials.

I almost made the All-Star lineup that year as a write-in, since I wasn't listed on the All-Star ballot. I had nearly 800,000 write-in votes in the fan balloting. The city of New York was behind me, and the press kept the pressure on Houk to get me more at-bats. The writers argued that a guy who was hitting around .400 should be playing every day.

Later that summer, I aggravated my hamstring again and my average began a steady fall over the final two months. I was moved back to the DH slot from first base, so my bat remained in the lineup most days. I managed to finish the year with a .329 average, seven points better than my average during my rookie season. Rod Carew's mark of .350 was the only better average in the A.L. that season. But with just 301 at-bats during the season, I didn't qualify for the batting title.

The designated hitter rule sparked controversy throughout the game. The National League hated it, and the American League loved it—and the two argued relentlessly about its worth. Some baseball men even flip-flopped on the subject. Sparky Anderson hated the rule when he was winning World Series titles in the N.L. with the Reds, but loved it when he later managed the Tigers. The same thing happened with Bobby Cox, who took a liking to the rule once he left the Braves for the Blue Jays. If the DH rule worked to a manager's favor, he probably liked it; if not, he couldn't stand the fact that baseball got away from its roots.

Some managers argued that the rule took away from the strategy of the game, doing away with a manager's need to pinch-hit for his pitcher and hence further reducing the need to substitute late in a game. But some players benefited mightily from the rule. Edgar Martinez became a six-time All-Star as a DH; Hall-of-Famer Paul Molitor played almost as many games as the DH as he did in the field; Reggie Jackson, Jim Rice, and Dave Winfield all prolonged their careers thanks to the rule; and in 1979, Don Baylor became the first player to spend significant time as a DH and still win an MVP award. Fans loved watching those players hit, as David Ortiz proved when the Red Sox won the World Series in 2004.

But not all players enjoyed time spent as a DH. For some who thought they deserved to play in the field, their ego got in the way. Others found the job a bore. Every DH has to develop his own routine: what do you do between at-bats if you're not playing in the field? I used to eat. It helped if the clubhouse had some food available, I spent a decent amount of time hanging out near the buffet table. Often, I would skip breakfast and just eat at the ballpark. I enjoyed getting my hits and then watching the rest of the game on TV or listening to it on the radio in the clubhouse. In my case, I had to interrupt my eating to hit. But my metabolism was high when I was a player, so I could get away with all that feasting. And believe me—I feasted. There was a restaurant with an all-you-can-eat buffet near our spring training complex called Chateau Madrid. I got tossed from there three or four times because I ate too much.

Maybe the DH rule has changed the history of the game, but no more so than people who use steroids, or tighter-wound balls, corked bats, or dinky ballparks. To paraphrase Roger

Kahn: ballplayers are still the boys of summer; they're just playing by different rules. With the designated hitter came a fresh era of change in the game. And the impact it had on my career was substantial. Some 30-plus years later, when I call to make reservations at a hotel or restaurant, people still recognize me: "Oh, yeah, Ron Blomberg, I remember that name. You were the first designated hitter in baseball." Fans remember me as not just someone who played baseball, but as a guy who *changed* baseball.

So today, I think the honor of being the first DH is far more special than I did on Opening Day in 1973. I may have made it into the Hall of Fame through the back door, but I'm still there. Looking back, I always thought baseball would eventually abolish the DH rule after a year or so. But the rule outlasted my career—and then some.

After my career was over, longtime sports journalist Dick Schaap told me, "Bloomie, there aren't too many 'firsts' in the world of baseball. You started an era that people love or they hate. They can never take away from you that you were the first DH." And I replied, "Yeah—Designated Hebrew!" He loved it.

Orlando Cepeda once said to me, "You took a career away from me." For many players—even great ones like Cepeda—their careers are forgotten. The fact that one at-bat earned me a lot of notoriety—not to mention a question in Trivial Pursuit—might be a bit unfair to others. But that's not for me to worry about. Besides, this book is about a first that is far more important than my being the first designated hitter. When I die, I'm going to have the following

inscribed on my tombstone: "Ron Blomberg, the first DH,
Designated Hebrew in the game of baseball."

This is my story.

2

BIG MAN IN LITTLE LEAGUE

I was born in Atlanta, Georgia, where my father, Sol, the son of Romanian immigrants, moved to from Asheville, North Carolina. He thought Atlanta presented better opportunities since it was a larger city. My mother, Goldie Rae, worked with my dad in his jewelry store on Alabama Street, where I hung out a lot as a kid. We lived in a middle-class neighborhood with only a handful of other Jews. So most of my friends, neighbors, and classmates were not Jewish. Only years later, when new businesses began to develop, did Atlanta attract a considerable Jewish population.

My trip to the big leagues began in the Deep South. As a kid, I played on teams that included few—if any—Jewish players. I knew maybe five or six good Jewish athletes, but they weren't serious athletes. They didn't *want* to develop their talents any further—to have a shot at a professional career. Their parents pushed them to become doctors or lawyers, or to enter the business world. Athletics were never considered a serious option for them. But my parents were different: they gave me the freedom to do what I wanted to do—to see how far my athletic ability would take me.

Many of my teammates were from lower-middle class families whose parents worked two jobs each. I helped out my family earning some extra money by delivering newspapers, selling Kool-Aid, and recycling bottles to collect the nickel deposit. But most of my free time was spent playing sports. I don't know where my athletic genes came from. No one in my family was athletic, so maybe I was a freak of nature. I ran a lot when I was younger and just naturally matured into a pretty strong kid.

I was strong mentally as well as physically. I had no choice, as growing up a young Southern Jew was not easy. In my late teen years, Lester Maddox, a former proponent of segregation, was the governor of Georgia. A synagogue firebombing occurred just three blocks from our house and made national headlines—as depicted in the movie *Driving Miss Daisy*. There were constant Ku Klux Klan marches, with Klansmen wearing their pointed hats and giving out pamphlets that were anti-Semitic, anti-black, and anti-Catholic. They used to march down Peachtree Street.

My religion even made playing the sport I loved a worrisome affair. On some of the little league teams I played on, plenty of my teammates didn't know what a "Jew" was. But some of them did, unfortunately, and they were Klansmen who regularly attended meetings and cross-burnings. They knew I was Jewish—on Rosh Hashanah and Yom Kippur, I went to services—but they never confronted me. As a gifted athlete and the team's best player, I was looked at as the savior of their team. Professional and college scouts came to our games to watch me play, and that gave teammates who were good enough a crack at athletic scholarships as well. So they never confronted me to my face, but I saw the KKK hoods and pamphlets in some of their parked cars. It was common to see a shotgun in someone's car, and I knew that after a game they might be headed to a cross-burning. It was intimidating at times.

But no amount of intimidation—whether direct or indirect—was going to keep me from being respectful of my religion and my parents' wishes. Growing up, I went to Hebrew School twice a week. Most Jewish kids disliked Hebrew School and tried to get out of attending, but I didn't mind going because I was proud of being Jewish. I often had to attend Hebrew School, hop in the car right afterward, change into my baseball uniform, and head to a game. I wasn't an Orthodox Jew, but I did observe the High Holy Days. I put on the *yarmulke* (a skull cap worn by Jews while in a temple) and *tallis* (a prayer shawl) and remained in synagogue all day long.

Of course, I was a kid, and so I screwed up from time to time. On one occasion when I was around the age of 12, I played golf with my cousin instead of observing Rosh Hashanah. I knew I was making a mistake, but I really wanted to hang out with him. My rabbi saw us on the golf course and told my parents, who reprimanded me. I felt bad about that poor judgment and never let it happen again.

My family believed in adhering to Jewish customs. We had a Seder every Passover. My parents would hide the *matzah* (a piece of unleavened bread) and I received 50 cents when I found it. But I had a hard time remaining as strict as my parents. I didn't remain kosher because I loved other foods. But I didn't think that made me a bad Jew. I was just never as religious a person as they were—but I wasn't ashamed of my religion.

Despite my small family, over 100 people attended my Bar Mitzvah. On my cake was a picture of me wearing a Yankee uniform complete with pinstripes. That was unheard of for a kid who grew up in the south, but I was pretty outspoken about wanting to play for the Yankees. Most of the gifts I received were of the sporting variety, including lots of baseball cards. Like most kids, I collected cards to put them in my bicycle spokes. Yankee players were my favorites; I had lots of Mickey Mantles and Art Ditmars.

I was never a fan of baseball, though. I was a *player*. I wanted to be like the guys in the major leagues, and I firmly believed that I could be like those guys. Whenever I played baseball in my front yard, I pretended that I was Mantle. I started playing organized ball at the age of eight, when I tried out for a Little League team. I was cut from the Sally League team but snuck back in with another number and made the team on my second try.

I was like The Hulk during my first year of Little League. Playing for the Levista Lions, I began my transformation from mere human to superhuman. My rate of improvement was remarkable. I didn't know how to throw a baseball properly, but I could throw as hard as anyone; I didn't know how to hit, but I was smacking line drives and home runs. The following season, at age nine, I made what they called the Major Leagues, an advanced form of Little League. Nobody *ever* made the major leagues at age nine. Most players at that level were 12 years old. I was a bit smaller than my teammates but still found success on the field. It was the start of a trend for me: Throughout my time in youth baseball, I was continually playing against older competition.

Even during my formative years in baseball, I knew that I wanted to make baseball my career. Making the major leagues was my goal, my fantasy, and my ambition. The coach who really helped me realize my dreams was Ralph Dorsey, my first coach in baseball. I remember him telling my mom and dad that I was "something else." I was nine years old and outperforming my older and bigger peers. And I was attracting a crowd at the ballpark.

Even though I batted lefthanded, I threw righthanded and played third base for my team, and pitched some, too. I was throwing seeds, as they say—striking a lot of batters out. I advanced to the Babe Ruth American Legion League and after I continued to show rapid improvement, I tried out for the Druid Hills High School team as a ninth grader. I made the varsity team, playing first and third base, and pitching. My high school was not a big baseball school at that time; we favored the football and basketball programs. Before the Atlanta Braves arrived in 1966, Atlanta's professional baseball team was the Crackers, a minor-league affiliate. So the town really didn't care much about baseball; it was no big deal. Most of the guys on my baseball team were football players who had signed football scholarships at different universities.

When I was in ninth grade, I met a scout from the Braves named Pucci Hartsfield, brother of Roy Hartsfield, who later became the first manager of the Toronto Blue Jays. Pucci had played for the Crackers and managed many minor-league teams, working for the Dodgers and Braves. He was the first professional scout to take an interest in me.

In tenth grade, I began playing basketball and developing a name for myself in that sport. I could jump like David Thompson—my vertical leap was recorded at 41 inches and I could dunk with ease. So I was playing above the rim as a young high schooler, which was something that nobody had ever seen a white guy do before. I was a six-foot center, but my height wasn't a big deal because I could jump so high to make up for my lack of size. I felt like a man playing against boys. I battled against plenty of black guys in pick-up games away from school, and that really helped me improve on the basketball court. At the time, our schools were segregated and whites did not play against blacks.

I lettered in all four sports in high school—baseball, basketball, football, and track—and I was successful at each. I was a wide receiver in football and ran the 100-yard dash in 9.4 seconds in track. But I never lost interest in baseball. My high school team wasn't that good, but I continued to play in the Babe Ruth league, as we had a super team. Scouts from the Dodgers, Braves, Indians, and Yankees were attending my games.

In a high school All-Star Game at the old Atlanta-Fulton County Stadium, I hit a home run on the second pitch of the game to straightaway center field, about 420 feet from home plate. After the game, Atley Donald, the same Yankee scout who signed Ron Guidry, told me he was going to recommend that the Yankees draft me.

I earned a lot of national publicity during my days at Druid Hills. In addition to articles in the local newspaper, wire services like the Associated Press and United Press International wrote articles about me. I was a first-team pick for *Parade* magazine's high school All-American team in both basketball and football. My high school basketball coach even told me that I was the best basketball player he had ever seen.

During my junior year, lots of colleges came calling, including Florida State, Florida, Alabama, USC, UCLA, Georgia, Arizona, Arizona State, Kentucky, and Tennessee. I had around 100 scholarship offers each to play college football and basketball, but far fewer baseball offers since baseball wasn't as prominent at that time. The schools offering me a baseball scholarship included Miami, Florida State, Florida, Miami Dade Junior College, Texas, USC, UCLA, Arizona, and Arizona State.

The attention was a bit overwhelming—I didn't know what to do. Some colleges even called my girlfriend and offered her a scholarship if I went to their school. Plus, I had an opportunity to play basketball at UCLA for legendary coach John Wooden, who actually came to Atlanta to scout both my teammate Rudy Kinard, a superb athlete who eventually committed to Tennessee, and me. I eventually signed a letter of intent to play basketball at UCLA, but that was before I realized I could make a whole lot of money immediately by playing professional baseball.

The Yankees had finished last in the American League in 1966, so they had first choice in the '67 amateur draft. Donald came through in his recommendation, and the Yankees made me the top pick in the country. There were lots of other good players available in that draft: Dusty Baker, Don Baylor, Bobby Grich, Jon Matlack, John Mayberry, Ken Singleton, Vida Blue, Ted Simmons, Steve Yeager, and Richie Zisk. I figured I would be taken in the top three, but when I heard I was going to the Yankees, I was elated. That changed my mind about attending college. I was a Yankee fan, and the opportunity to play for my favorite team was too good to pass up.

When I signed my baseball contract, it voided every college scholarship offer I had received. Today, things would be different: if I signed to play professional baseball, I could still play college football or basketball. I did enroll at DeKalb Junior College and attended classes during the off-season for one semester. I later enrolled at Fairleigh Dickinson University, in Teaneck, New Jersey, as a psychology major. But I regret that I never experienced regular life on a college campus. Still today I'm a huge college football and basketball fan and enjoy going to games with my son at the University of Miami and my daughter at the University of Alabama.

While I missed out on college, however, I'm so glad that I didn't miss out on playing for the Yankees.

3

THE NEXT MICKEY MANTLE

Before the Milwaukee Braves moved to Atlanta in 1966, baseball was just not big in the southeast. The southernmost clubs in the east were the Baltimore Orioles and the Washington Senators. But as a kid in Atlanta, we did get baseball's "Game of the Week" broadcast on television. More often than not, it was a Yankees game. That was just fine with my dad, who rooted for the team, and with me, who followed suit.

I was a fan of the Yankees in general and Mickey Mantle in particular. I think he was the favorite player of almost everybody—kid or adult—who rooted for the Yankees. I collected his cards and imitated his hitting stance when I was at the plate. I wasn't a switch-hitter like Mickey, but whenever I batted, I did my best to look like a lefthanded Mickey Mantle. I hit quite a few home runs pretending to be Mantle, so at times I really felt like I *was* him.

I must have hit enough like him to be worth a big gamble for the Yankees, who signed me for $105,000, which at the time was an awful lot of money.

Being a Jewish athlete and a guy who loved the big city, New York was the only place to play sports. It was a great opportunity for me. Before I even signed my contract, many New Yorkers were contacting me, begging me to play in the Big Apple. They wrote to me: "We need you. We want you to be our Messiah." The fans of New York were hungry for a star Jewish player to represent them.

The Yankees were not a very good team in the mid-to-late Sixties. After acquiring Babe Ruth from the Red Sox in 1920, the Yankees won 20 World Series titles and 29 pennants over the next 44 years. CBS purchased the team in 1964, and in 1965 the team posted the first of three straight losing seasons. They were bottom-dwellers in 1966 and '67, and attendance was dropping off. Team president Mike Burke realized that having a Jewish star in New York could really help at the turnstiles. Teaming up with general manager Lee MacPhail and Johnny Johnson, Burke negotiated with my father and me, begging me to sign. The day after I graduated from high school, the same scout who had recommended me to the Yankees, Atley Donald, flew down to Atlanta and signed me in a hotel near the airport.

As a Jewish ballplayer in Atlanta, I didn't receive much coverage related to my religion. But I knew that things would change in New York City. After I signed, the Yankees flew me up to New York with my parents for a press conference and a get-acquainted tour. I had never been on an airplane before. Nor had I ever even *seen* a limousine, which took us from the airport to the hotel. I was all wide-eyed, especially when I saw the marquee of the New York Hilton. It read: WELCOME, FIRST-ROUND DRAFT PICK OF THE NEW YORK YANKEES, RON BLOMBERG.

The fellow who checked me in at the Hilton was a Jewish man named Mort, who turned out to be a big memorabilia collector. When he was introduced to me, he said, "Ah, a *lantzman*," meaning a fellow Jew. I signed something for him, probably the first time I was asked for an autograph.

We checked in and they carried my bags. I had an entourage, maybe 25 or 30 people met me in the lobby, most of them Jewish people wearing *yarmulkes*. Some of them were Hasidic Jews. I had never seen a Hasidic Jew prior to that day. I was so naïve—I thought they looked like Pilgrims.

Even the taxi driver who took me to the stadium was Jewish. When I mentioned my name, he said, "You're the baseball player." It was a wonderful feeling; it seemed like everyone knew who I was and was expecting me. When I went to The Stage deli, they put my picture up on the wall and I became very good friends with the owner. I sat in the seat where Joe DiMaggio used to sit and was served by the same waitress, Cleo, who had served Joltin' Joe. I ate a corned beef sandwich that must have weighed 12 ounces. Later, The Stage even named a sandwich after me. It was a reuben, with corned beef, pastrami, cheese, and Russian dressing.

The Yankees then took us to Toots Shor's, where all the big players hung out. Toots came over and sat down with us. I didn't know who he was at the time, but of course later on I found out that he was a real big guy on the New York sports scene. The team wasn't finished rolling out the red carpet, yet. We were given front-row tickets to see Zero Mostel in *Fiddler on the Roof*. After the performance, as the cast was introduced to the audience, the announcer said, "We want to welcome Ron Blomberg, the first-round draft pick of the New York Yankees." Everybody in the place stood up and applauded, which gave me goose bumps. Then we were escorted backstage to meet Mostel.

The grand finale was yet to come, however. At Yankee Stadium, my reception was even warmer. I was interviewed by Walter Cronkite, who was in the broadcast booth with Phil Rizzuto. I remembered seeing him on TV, but I never watched the news. I was 18 years old and Walter Cronkite shook my hand and sat down with me for an interview. That was my first major interview with anybody in New York City. The date was June 20, 1967.

I was in hog heaven. I visited the monuments beyond the outfield wall. Then I dressed in a uniform and they had a special food spread for me. Pete Sheehy retrieved my uniform, No. 12, and said he would take care of it for me. "When you come up here," he told me, "this will be yours." Then he started talking about all the great ballplayers who had come through there: Babe Ruth, Lou Gehrig, Joe DiMaggio, and Mickey Mantle. He was like a father to me and really eased my transition from high school to the big leagues.

I hit some long home runs in batting practice and said to myself, "Golly, Pete, this is wonderful." There were lots of stars hanging around during batting practice. Yogi Berra and Whitey Ford showed up, and Mickey was there too, along with Mel

Stottlemyre, manager Ralph Houk, and coaches Elston Howard, Dick Howser, and Jim Turner. They all wanted to see what the hype was about. Everyone was so nice to me, and they shook my hand and welcomed me to the Yankees.

The Yankees were playing Detroit that day, and the team placed a sign on the scoreboard that read: WELCOME FIRST-ROUND DRAFT PICK RON BLOMBERG. I was watching the game in the broadcast booth with Rizzuto, and the fans in the grandstand stood up and applauded in our general direction. Rizzuto told me to wave to them, so I did, and they cheered louder. I was living a dream. God gave me three wishes, and the first one was to play in Yankee Stadium.

I sure made the ushers happy. Most of them were Jewish, with names like Hymowitz or Lichstein, and three or four of them told me they never thought they would ever see a Jew play baseball in Yankee Stadium. They had tears in their eyes and said to me, "You little Yid, you're someone I can look up to now. Thank you for coming."

There were no other Jewish ballplayers on the Yankees. The Yankees had Bob Fishel and Marty Appel in the public relations department, and Howard Berk was vice president for administration, but that was it.

Standing in Yankee Stadium that day, donning a uniform and listening to the sound of the bat hitting the ball was an odd sensation. I felt closed in. I was used to playing in yards, but now I was playing professional baseball. It was just an unbelievable sensation. But the bubble burst quickly: the next day, I headed back to Atlanta with my parents, and began packing for my first minor-league assignment in Johnson City, Tennessee.

The Yankees team in Johnson City was a Rookie League farm club managed by Dick Berardino, a former minor-league player and the brother of John Berardino, star of the television soap opera *General Hospital*. There were a lot of No. 1 draft choices in that league: Bobby Grich, Jon Matlack, Don Baylor, and Wayne Twitchell. I was just out of high school and nervous as could be, but my uncle, Mitchell Thorpe, calmed me down. He was the mayor of Johnson City. Uncle Mitch did a lot for the city and he loved baseball. In fact, he owned part of the team. It helped that he was there since I had never been away from home before.

I flew to Johnson City in a two-engine airplane and my uncle came out to meet me, as did the news media. There were a slew of people taking pictures and asking for interviews. It was two or three days before the season started but we had to have a press conference to accommodate all the press people from all across the region who showed up. I had dinner with my uncle at his house, and more reporters showed up there, too. They interviewed me for a feature for the Sunday paper and took more pictures. All this happened before I had even met any of my teammates.

I roomed with a pitcher, Doug Hansen, who got drafted out of Fresno State. We became fast friends. Several of my teammates had played minor-league baseball before, so being 18 and without any experience made for a rough transition. The roster was always in flux—three guys would be added, and three more removed, then the following week a new batch would arrive. The locker room was like a game of musical chairs.

When I arrived that first day, I received the cold stare from many of my teammates, who wondered why I was receiving the royal treatment. Low-round draft picks only received $250 to sign and were making $500 a month. Everyone made $500 a month; it didn't matter who you were. It was a lot of money at the time, and I thought it was great.

The paparazzi were present for my first game. My teammates continued their standoffish attitude toward me. I don't blame them; it was as if Joe DiMaggio or Mickey Mantle were playing first base for Johnson City instead of Ron Blomberg. I could have done without the added attention, and on top of all the cameras and press, the game was sold out. For me, playing professional baseball was already a little bit scary. I was the best in each of the sports I played in high school, so everybody looked at me as a phenom. But even at the Rookie League level, I found pro ball a lot different than playing in high school. Suddenly, the talent level all around me was significantly better; my prowess on the field was no longer quite so obvious.

In my first at-bat I faced Wayne Twitchell, who pitched for a team managed by Whitey Herzog. Twitchell threw really hard, and I was intimidated. But I drew a walk—just as I did years later in my first at-bat as a designated hitter. My second time up, I hit a home run over the right-field lights, finally breaking the ice with my teammates. I remember circling the bases and feeling a ton of pressure lift off my shoulders. There were plenty of handshakes and high-fives waiting for me in the dugout.

Although I had signed as an outfielder, I was playing first base because that's where the Yankees thought I would best fit into their lineup. They were in need of a successor to Mantle,

who played first base late in his career. I actually felt more comfortable in right field and did a good job out there when given
the chance. I had a real good season in Johnson City, and our
team finished second in the division. I hit about .295 with 12 or
13 home runs during the short-season schedule. I made the All-
Star team and became good friends with the guys on the team.
Other than Rusty Torres and Cesar Geronimo, we didn't have a
lot of guys on that team who went on to make the major
leagues. But we did have quite a few who reached the Triple-A
level. Rusty and Cesar gave my confidence a big boost when
they told me they had never seen a sweeter swing than mine.
That meant a lot to me. I had the respect of the guys on the team
and the respect of the city. And my uncle and his family took real
good care of me during my time in Johnson City.

As a Jew playing in a small, southern town, I was a novelty. There wasn't a lot of understanding in the rural south. Most
people knew about Hebrews from Bible study, and everybody
knew that Jesus was a Jew. But comprehension ended right
there. I honestly think some people were surprised that I didn't
have horns. On occasion, I heard phrases like "Jew boy," "Jewin'
me," or "Jew me down" (when talking about money). But I
never confronted anyone. I knew they were just uneducated
about my religion and didn't know what they were talking
about. They had heard those words from their parents or
friends, and were simply conforming to what they had already
experienced. The words hurt, but I couldn't risk any confronta-
tions.

That winter, the Yankees sent me to their Instructional
League team in Clearwater, Florida. My season had lasted just

three months in Johnson City and I got only 200 at-bats. The Yankees wanted to see their top prospects get more seasoning. I entered the 1968 season full of optimism, and upon being granted a ticket to the Yankees major-league spring training camp as a non-roster invitee, my confidence was boosted even further. Being a hot-shot "bonus baby"—as they once called players who received a large signing bonus upon being drafted—I was assigned to room with Mickey Mantle in spring training. Players always had roommates in those days, and the entire team stayed in a hotel called The Yankee Clipper. When I was casually informed that I was rooming with Mantle, I replied, "Nah, no way am I rooming with Mickey Mantle." But there it was on the rooming list: Blomberg and Mantle. If Neil Simon hadn't adopted the idea first, then Mickey and I would've been The Odd Couple: the Jewish teenager from the South and the fading superstar from Oklahoma.

We weren't truly roommates in the sense that we shared a room. Rather, we shared a wall and a door. We had adjacent rooms with an adjoining door. If I opened that door, I could walk into his room. At the stadium the first day of spring training, I saw Mickey getting a rubdown on the training table. I walked over and said, "Mickey, we're rooming together." He just looked at me blankly and didn't respond. I was out on the field thinking, "Gosh, I'm going to room with Mickey." But Mickey was carrying on pretty well at that particular point in his career, so he spent little time in his room. He was a phantom, and his room was simply for storing his luggage. The only time I ever saw him was at the ballpark.

By 1968, his career was pretty much over. He had but one year left, and he would retire at the age of 37. In his prime, he was a great athlete, but he suffered through debilitating injuries, and coupled with his drinking and carousing, his career was possibly cut a bit short. Yankees clubhouse attendant Pete Sheehy had to keep doling out bicarbonates to remedy Mickey's hangovers. His knees were all taped up and it was hard for him to get off the table and walk around. But I looked past that. Mickey was wonderful to me. I have pictures of him teaching me to play the outfield. His form of teaching was certainly unique: "Just watch me do it," he would say. Everything came so naturally to him.

My first locker was right next to Mickey's locker, which was a deliberate move on the team's part. They wanted the old Mickey Mantle right next to whom they viewed as the new Mickey Mantle—me. I was hoping to do the same thing for jersey No. 12 that Mickey did for No. 7. I thought I had a good chance to make the club in my first spring, but it was not to be. I was sent down to the minor-league camp in Hollywood, Florida, to finish out spring training. The rest of the spring went well, and I was sent packing for the Yankees' minor-league team in Kinston, North Carolina. Kinston was a town in the eastern portion of the state—not too far away from Morehead City and the ocean—in a region known for its tobacco. The league was Single-A but had a reputation for good baseball. Unfortunately, I didn't live up to the standard of the league that season, partly due to Uncle Sam's bequest.

By 1968, I was eligible for a *different* draft: the United States military. The Vietnam War was raging then, and I was placed into a National Guard unit in Atlanta. It was a special outfit with a lot of professional football and basketball players, doctors, pilots, and even a few future politicians. One of them was Rankin Smith Jr., whose father owned the NFL's Atlanta Falcons for many years.

The Yankees saw to it that I was included in this unique National Guard unit. I was glad—I was fresh out of high school, already in a strange land in the minor leagues, and I didn't want to go to war. At that time, my baseball career had a huge upside, and I didn't want anything to interfere with that potential. Plenty of other athletes were in the same boat with me, fulfilling their military obligation by serving in the National Guard. It wasn't fun.

I felt like I was leading two lives: baseball prospect and soldier in training. The National Guard required one weekend a month and two weeks in the summer for six years. It was no problem during the off-season but definitely gave me problems during the season. I was being shipped back home to Atlanta once a month for my mandatory National Guard duty. On the weekend of my training, I would leave early Friday morning, fly home on one of those prop airplanes, then get up early on Saturday to make my training. On Monday, I'd fly back to wherever my team was playing at that time.

Even though it was just once a month, the trip was a huge disruption. I was used to playing baseball every day—staying in a rhythm—and missing four or five days just threw my rhythm out of whack. Each time I would return it was like going through spring training all over again; I found it very difficult and had a hard time adjusting to the routine. Things worsened when I was sent to Fort Jackson, South Carolina, for six months of basic training in the middle of the season. When I arrived, the first thing I learned was that 98 percent of the people stationed at Fort Jackson—inner-city kids who were drafted—would be going to Vietnam. They hated the Army Reserve and the National Guard.

My first couple days served as an ample introduction to life in training—life without any of the perks I had grown accustomed to since graduation. I was crammed along with 200 others into trucks that took us to a reception center. There I was asked what I wanted to eat and then told I would have to sleep at the center because I had arrived too late to be assigned to a unit that day. I was then told that I could "sleep late" the next day. I thought to myself, "Gee, this isn't so bad."

At three o'clock in the morning, all of the men stranded at the center were forced to run all the way to Fort Jackson. Breakfast—just some slop—was then served and I was assigned to a unit. Then the drill sergeants arrived to inspect each unit, demanding us to stand at attention while they walked down the line, shoving us and kicking us. These guys had just returned from Vietnam, and I honestly didn't know if they had all of their senses working. They were muscular guys with shaved heads and big hats—pretty scary-looking. Once their "inspection" was over, we were ordered to run some more. I was in pretty good shape, but everybody else was ready to collapse, so the drill sergeants kicked them some more and made them go into the grease pits. I thought, "What have I gotten myself into?"

These drill sergeants were remarkable characters. They would get in your face, ridicule you, spit on you, whatever it took to intimidate you. They were tough: guys with tattoos who talked about drugs and were big drinkers. We didn't know if they were messed up on drugs or not, but they talked about marijuana, heroin, and LSD. Each morning, when they had to wake us up and run us around, many of them had rings under their eyes and looked nasty—probably suffering from hangovers. Halfway into the session, one of my platoon leaders went off into the woods and started shooting into the air. He thought he was back in Vietnam. The military police intervened, locking him up.

There was no limit to their intensity or cruelty. One time, two Hispanic guys who bunked near me got up at four o'clock in the morning and started fighting with knives. As punishment, they made all of us polish our platoon room. We thought it was predictable when the drill sergeant came in to expect our work, spat on the floor, and made us do it again.

After a very rough three or four weeks, though, the commanding officer found out that I was a professional athlete. The commander sent word that he wanted to see me. Three other men, two football players and a baseball player, were also summoned. We were asked to play on the platoon baseball team with the commander of the whole post. From that point on, life became a little easier at Fort Jackson. Whenever other men were doing physical training, I was playing baseball, basketball, or flag football. After I helped our team win the post baseball championship, I was thanked and congratulated by the commander. Winning wasn't that easy, however, because we played against professional athletes from other divisions. We *had* to win.

Basic training lasted three months. After that, I had to complete another three months of Advanced Individual Training, also at Fort Jackson. I had never typed before in my life, but they made me a clerk-typist. I sat there in front of a typewriter with no clue how to type. My instructors asked why a big lug like me was doing something like that. I told them that was the Military Occupational Specialty I was given. Maybe it was somebody's idea of a joke, since I typed 10 words a minute.

At Fort Jackson, I tried to keep my religion to myself—for the first time in my life. In my downtime the memory of those Ku Klux Klan rallies and synagogue bombings from my youth crept up on me. Some of the guys went to church services on Sunday so they could get out of some of their duties, but I wasn't about to follow suit. I didn't want the people I hung around with to know that I was Jewish, because I was afraid for my safety. I was surrounded by extreme men, and I wasn't protected. Somebody might "accidentally" lose their aim on the firing range or even pull a grenade pin in my proximity. I thought about that many, many times, knowing I was often sitting next to people who were not real stable. I remember my drill sergeant addressing me on one occasion: "You a Jew?" he asked me. Stupid me—he was a drill sergeant and I said, "Yes, sir." You don't say "sir" to a drill sergeant, so he made me do extra push-ups.

After completing my basic training, I headed back home and fell back into my familiar routine: One weekend a month was spent in National Guard training, and two weeks of the summer was spent in summer camp. It was miserable, but I did it for six years as part of an air surveillance unit.

I didn't have a real good season in Kinston due in part to my National Guard duty. But I do have some fond memories of my time there. I was always known as a major eater, and with good reason. In fact, one of my baseball cards even said that I ate 28 McDonald's hamburgers at one sitting because somebody bet me I couldn't do it. That actually happened when I was still in high school. A nearby McDonald's offered a free hamburger to anyone who had a 1956 penny. I had 28 of them, and cashed them all in at the same time. That was one heck of a dinner.

We didn't have a lot of money when I was growing up, so I had to make the most of my opportunities. I loved smorgasbords, especially ones that offered shrimp and prime rib. And I could eat two large pizzas in one sitting. My appetite was legendary throughout Atlanta; the *Atlanta Journal-Constitution* even wrote a story about my eating prowess.

The press picked up on that angle when I arrived in Kinston, and word soon spread throughout the town that I was good with the bat—and with a fork and knife. There was a restaurant in Kernersville, North Carolina, that offered a 72-ounce steak free of charge *if* you could eat it in an hour. The steak was gigantic—like a half a leg, with no fat on it. And you also had to have a salad, three vegetables, and dessert. If you couldn't do it, the price was $25, big money in those days. I enjoyed that meal on three occasions, and never opened my wallet. The first time it took me only half an hour.

While my legend at the supper table was meeting expectations, my work on the diamond was still cut out for me.

4

GETTING THE CALL

After a good spring training with the Yankees in 1969, I was sent to the Double-A affiliate in Manchester, New Hampshire, where Jerry Walker was the manager. He was a former major-league pitcher and a super manager. In my second year of commuting back and forth because of my military obligation, I endured the transitions better and put together a solid season. I played left field—where I showcased my arm by leading the league in assists—and made the Eastern League All-Star team. I hit .284 with 19 homers in 107 games, good enough to get called up to New York at the end of the year. Less than a month after my 21st birthday, I made my major-league debut, on September 10, 1969, getting a walk as a pinch-hitter. I wound up collecting three singles in six at-bats but made a good first impression with a batting-practice home run that went over the roof of Tiger Stadium in Detroit.

Still the Yankees didn't think I was ready. During 1970 spring training, I thought I had a shot at the job. I got a lot of at-bats and had a spectacular spring. I was crushing the ball on a consistent basis. Opposing managers and players were watching me. One day, before a game in Pompano Beach, Ted Williams, then the manager of the Washington Senators, came up to me at the cage and said, "You've got a great stroke. Keep it up." Williams had a reputation for disliking rookies, who did not enjoy playing for him. Though Williams made me feel pretty special that day, the feeling didn't last long.

Back in Fort Lauderdale, I was shagging flies in the outfield on the final day of spring training when I saw clubhouse attendant Pete Sheehy out of the corner of my eye. Everybody knew that Pete would come to get you if you were being sent down. I thought maybe about trying to hide from him. Pete told me that manager Ralph Houk wanted to see me, and right then I knew I was being demoted. I was disappointed. "There's no way I'm going to make this team," I thought to myself. "I'm 21 years old and we have all these guys who are 30 or 35."

I remember going into Ralph's office, and all the front office personnel were there—Lee MacPhail, Johnny Johnson, and Mike Burke. Ralph said, "I just want you to know that you will be up here for many, many years. You've done great this spring, and you are our hope for the future. What we want you to do is play first base. We've already got a first baseman (Danny Cater) so we are going to send you down to Triple-A. But we're going to watch every move you make and we'll call you up real quick if we need you."

That was my "Dear John" letter. I went back into the clubhouse, where Pete had already packed my bags. He sat down with me and said, "I've been around the best. I want you to be one of the best. You have that opportunity. I've been watching you. You have great ability and you bring a lot of excitement to the game of baseball." He hugged me and told me that I would be in the major leagues for a long time.

I left for the Triple-A squad in Syracuse, where Frank Verdi was the manager. It seemed like everybody was even older there than the guys on the big-league roster. They were all nice, but some of those guys already had kids, and I didn't know any of them because none of them had been in big-league camp. Most of the other guys who were sent down from big-league camp went to A-ball or Double-A. I was the only 21-year-old on that team.

Triple-A was a new experience for me. The manager didn't give me any preferential treatment. Matter of fact, I grabbed some pine during our season opener, which upset me. But I got my chance to play soon enough, just not at first base.

In a radio interview, Frank Verdi announced he was going to put me in right field because Tony Solaita—who could hit the long ball—was going to play first base. Frank was an Old School guy. He never smiled and he loved the older players. They played cards together and went out drinking every night. I didn't play cards and didn't drink, so in short, I didn't fit in. Frank hardly spoke to me. I was supposed to be the organization's favorite guy—the top prospect—and he was from Long Island, so I'm sure he saw all the articles about me during the off-season. But he never showed that he liked me. He probably wanted to put somebody older in right field; maybe he felt like he was stuck with me. But the lack of emotion he displayed was unsettling. To say the least, I was scared.

I batted fifth or sixth in the batting order, and I was off to a decent start when my military obligation interrupted my season again, forcing me to leave for two-week summer camp. A couple of my teammates went to Fort Drum in Watertown, New York, which was a hop, skip, and a jump from Syracuse. They came back for games. But not me. Once again, I had to go back to Atlanta, which made things really difficult. Unfortunately, transferring units wasn't an option, either.

When I returned to the team, Frank benched me for my first game back. Then, all of a sudden, he decided to start platooning me against lefthanders, giving me the night off if we were facing a lefty starter. I said to myself, "What in the world is going on?" I wound up hitting about .270 that year, and I did well in right field. But the season was still frustrating.

But relief was on the way. After spending all of 1970 in the minors, I finally reached the big leagues to stay in 1971. I began the season in the minors, however, with instructions to work on my defense at first base. Loren Babe, a low-key, well-mannered guy, had replaced Frank Verdi as the manager in Syracuse. But just like Verdi, Babe benched me against lefthanded pitchers. I was hitting well over .300, but Loren still wouldn't let me hit against lefthanders. I was perplexed—and frustrated—because I had hit lefties well my whole life. All he would tell me in response was, "Your time will come."

Well, he was sort of right about that. By June, I had proved to the Yankees that I was ready for the call. I played my first game of the season for New York on June 25, getting the start in right field instead of first base. In the third inning, I hit my first major league home run to right-center off Senators pitcher Pete

Broberg, a two-run shot that knocked him out of the game. The homer sailed over the bullpen in the old Yankee Stadium, and must have traveled at least 425 feet. Two innings later I doubled and scored, making me two-for-five in my first game of the season. There were plenty of congratulations directed my way in the dugout during that game; I even received a handshake from Houk, who would soon become a point of frustration for me.

My impressive debut started up the hype machine once again. In the papers, I was again referred to as "the next Mickey Mantle"—big shoes to fill indeed. Even though the team was playing poorly, I was a point of interest for reporters, who flocked to my locker after games. There would be more of that in years to come: I liked to talk, so I became a favorite amongst the press.

I also liked to eat. On the way home from Yankee Stadium after one afternoon game that summer, I stopped for a snack—even though I had made plans to go out to dinner at 7:30 that night. It was six o'clock and I was hungry, so I ate two hamburgers, two steak sandwiches, a hot dog, two sides of potato salad, and washed it down with a pitcher of iced tea. Then I went out to dinner and had a full-course steak dinner. Sounds unbelievable, I know. But it's true. I couldn't eat that way now, but as a 23-year-old I had an amazing metabolism. I never put on much weight.

On the field, I was feasting on opposing pitchers. I was off to a hot start in my first real crack at the majors, hitting .357 through my first 20 games. I hadn't hit against lefthanders in two years in the minors, so Ralph Houk continued to platoon me. I wouldn't say the manager's decision ruined my career, but it definitely held me back. They had hyped me up as the next superstar, but I was confused as to why a superstar would be platooned. Possibly, they wanted a star *Jewish* player, and not a star *baseball* player. I couldn't see what they had to lose in allowing me to play every day. The pennant wasn't exactly on the line in the early '70s: those clubs were struggling to finish .500 on the season. Still, I never rocked the boat. I never demanded, "Play me or trade me." We all had one-year contracts then, and I for one didn't want management to be upset with me—they held too much sway over my future.

Houk was an old-school manager who was conditioned to do things by the book. The book stated that lefthanded hitters usually have trouble hitting lefthanded pitchers. But that was not always the case. Babe Ruth wasn't platooned simply because he batted lefthanded. Neither was Ted Williams, Stan Musial, or Eddie Mathews. I don't mean to compare myself to a list of Hall of Famers, but how would I ever know if I compared favorably to them unless I was given the chance? That's all I wanted: an opportunity to prove Ralph wrong.

Houk—who stuck to his reasoning when it suited him, but abandoned it at other times—handled the situation poorly. Using his rationale, I should have played first base in New York because I played first base for Syracuse. But instead, I made all of my starts my rookie season in right field. Danny Cater, Johnny Ellis, and Felipe Alou—an early-season acquisition—shared first base duties for the '71 Yankees. None of them set the world on fire, but I had a good year, hitting .322 with seven home runs. The team finished fourth in the American League East, 21 games behind the Baltimore Orioles.

Our most memorable game came in the season finale at Washington—a game I didn't even appear in. It was the Senators' final game in Washington; they were set to move to Texas in the off-season. We were losing 7-5 going into the top of the ninth inning. Alou grounded out to begin the inning, and Bobby Murcer followed suit with a groundout for the inning's second out. With just one out left to get, Washington fans stormed the field, hoping for a souvenir from the field. The game wasn't over yet, but the umpires had no option but to declare a forfeit. The game went into the books as a win for the Yankees, even though the Senators had been leading at the time play was stopped. All stats counted from the game, but there was no winning or losing pitcher of record.

The best thing about that game was that it propelled the Yankees above .500, at 82-80. Our record reflected the team's mediocrity. We had an average pitching staff and an average lineup. The team received most of its production from left fielder Roy White—who hit .292 with 19 homers—and 25-year-old center-fielder Bobby Murcer, who enjoyed the best season of his career by posting a .331 average and hitting 25 home runs. All five members of our rotation—Mel Stottlemyre, Fritz Peterson, Stan Bahnsen, Steve Kline, and Mike Kekich—won in double figures. But the bullpen was in poor shape, convincing the club to trade Cater to Boston for Sparky Lyle the following spring.

I guess I looked good in pinstripes. Maybe that was the reason I was asked to appear in the baseball drama *Bang the Drum Slowly*, which starred Robert De Niro as a terminally ill catcher who is forced to deal with his impending death during his final season on the team. The film crew took footage of me catching a fly ball in right-center field. I remember them coming out to the stadium to shoot the movie and telling me they had filmed me catching the ball. But I never earned a penny off that catch. I eventually saw the movie in Ridgewood, New Jersey with my agent, Sheldon Stone, and our wives.

Endorsements and commercials were on the horizon for me. Fielding offers wasn't a problem; fielding my position was, however. The Yankees considered me their first baseman of the future, so they sent me to the Instructional League to yet again work on my defense. Bill White, a Yankee broadcaster who had been a seventime Gold Glove winner at first base, was assigned to work with me. I told him that I liked playing the outfield because I needed the freedom to walk around between pitches and batters. My English teacher once called me a "heebee jeebee," a person always active or talking to people. I couldn't even keep still during the National Anthem. I just had a lot of energy to burn.

I also learned a lot from Bill, namely that playing first base is a lot different than playing the outfield. In the outfield, the ball comes to you in the air. At first base, it comes to you at 100 miles per hour. The outfield was easier for me because of my speed and my throwing arm. I didn't have a real easy time adjusting to the infield. I had to make sidearm throws to second base, and I was to used to throwing over the top. Some fans think a guy can move to first base, catch the ball, and be on his way. But it's not so easy. Playing first requires significant adjustments to a player's footwork and reaction time. A pitcher's throw to first base to check on a runner is difficult because it has additional movement on it. I could not have been a catcher for that reason. When Sparky Lyle was on the mound, his pitches danced all over the place. I hated when Sparky threw me the ball because it was so difficult to catch.

The hardest play for me at first base was fielding a grounder and throwing to second. A couple of my throws actually drilled the baserunner in the head. I was aiming for his head because that's what I was trained to do as an outfielder: whenever I had to throw to the cutoff guy, I aimed for his head. Errant throws like that began my reputation as a bad fielder, but all things considered I thought I was pretty good with the glove. But changing positions wasn't easy for me. Mickey Mantle and Hank Aaron also had a hard time moving from the outfield to first base late in their careers.

Bill kept telling me, "You're never going to make it." But I was good enough to get by. Besides, the Yankees liked me for my hitting, and I crushed the ball during my rookie campaign, and continued to do so in the Instructional League. We played doubleheaders every day, arriving at the park at eight or 8:30 in the morning and heading home around five in the afternoon. It was a lot of work, but it was worth it if I could show the Yankees any improvement in the field.

———————————

The 1972 season was going to be my first full year in the major leagues, and I wanted to take advantage of it. But it got off to a bad start: When players and owners couldn't come to terms on a new collective bargaining agreement—the argument between the two sides hinged on player pensions and salary arbitration—the players went on strike at the start of the season that lasted 13 days.

Once the season finally began in mid-April, I enjoyed a relatively productive season, making it into more games (107) and hitting more home runs (14) than in any other year in my career. But my bad shoulder kept my batting average down; I hit only .268 despite posting a solid on-base and slugging percentage. As was a trend in my career, I walked more often than I struck out. In 299 at-bats that season, I struck out just 26 times. In '72, I also made a relatively successful transition from right field to first base.

But due to my nagging physical problems and Houk's reluctance to play me against lefthanded pitchers, I still wasn't a regular for the Yankees. Had I played more frequently, the Yankees might have finished first in a weak division. We wound up fourth for the second consecutive season, but finished only six and a half games behind the first-place Detroit Tigers, who won the division by a half-game over the Boston Red Sox. Other than Murcer, who hit 33 homers, and Lyle, who had 35 saves in his first season in New York, the '72 Yankees didn't have much to brag about on an individual level. The rotation was solid again—Kline posted a 16-9 record and a 2.40 ERA—and the pen was improved, but our offense wasn't potent enough to carry us to a division title. My 14 home runs were second on the team; Roy White was the only other Yankee to reach double digits in homers with 10.

But there was at least one hint on that '72 team as to what to expect in the future. Catcher Thurman Munson notched his third season behind the plate as a 25-year-old, hitting .280 with 46 RBI. The following year, he would break out in a big way, following up on the success of his Rookie of the Year campaign in 1970. More important, however, big changes were right around the corner in the front office. A new boss was arriving to steer the Yankees back to the winning tradition they had grown accustomed to since the 1920s.

5

THE YIDDISH YANKEE

When I was a kid, most of my friends did not believe that a Jewish player could make it in the major leagues. Sandy Koufax and Hank Greenberg had done it, but they were viewed as exceptions. My friends thought that I was crazy for wanting to be a baseball player. Most of my Jewish friends planned on becoming doctors or lawyers. I was different: I wanted to be a baseball player, and that made me a curiosity in my crowd.

Not only did I want to be a professional baseball player, but I wanted to play for the Yankees, which made my desire all the more peculiar. Although the New York Giants and Brooklyn Dodgers were eager to tap the city's large Jewish population by bringing in Jewish players, the Yankees didn't seem interested. They had also been slow to sign a black player, adding Elston Howard a full eight years after Jackie Robinson had broken baseball's color line in 1947.

At different periods during the 1920s through the 1960s, the Giants roster included Andy Cohen, Harry Danning, and Sid Gordon, while the Dodgers featured Goody Rosen, Cal Abrams, and the biggest of all Jewish stars, Koufax. Hank Greenberg, who became a Hall of Fame first baseman for the Detroit Tigers, was *from* New York but didn't play for a New York team. With Lou Gehrig at first base, the Yankees passed on Greenberg, a star in their own backyard from James Monroe High School in the Bronx. All the way back to the regime of Col. Jacob Ruppert, who owned the team during the Babe Ruth era, the Yankees had maintained a corporate "WASPish" image that excluded Jews. Until I made my major league debut in 1969, the only Jewish player to ever don the pinstripes was Jimmie Reese, a utility infielder who once roomed with Ruth. Reese had hidden his Jewish identity by changing his name, which was really James Herman Solomon.

Reese was not above sharing his true religious background on one occasion, however. He had such great success against a pitcher that the catcher that day asked him point blank if he knew what pitches were coming. The pitcher and catcher, both also Jewish, had been communicating their signals verbally in Yiddish. Jimmie looked down at the catcher and said, "I'll tell you a secret. My real name is Hymie Solomon."

I remember meeting Jimmie in his old age when he was a coach for the Angels. I'll never forget what he said. He came up to me and said, "How do you like living in New York? Isn't being Jewish and living in New York the best thing in the world?"

I didn't have much of a Jewish identity myself until I arrived in New York. But that changed quickly. The Yankees were a middling team when I signed and began to establish myself in the late Sixties and early Seventies. The media wrote of me as the great hope of the future, and so I became popular with fans. The Jewish fans made me feel especially welcome—both on and off the field.

Growing up down South, being Jewish meant you held Jewish beliefs, but you didn't necessarily practice the religion. Upon my arrival in New York City, I felt an incredibly intense, brand new connection to my religion: I felt as if I were one of the chosen, simply because of how I was viewed and treated by the city's Jewish population. I was easy to spot—thin, with blond hair and blue eyes. I often wore Izod t-shirts, which were popular then. When I walked to and from the stadium before and after a game, fans were very friendly to me, waving or asking for autographs. Most fans knew that I stayed at the Concourse Plaza in the Bronx, and they were familiar with my route to and from the stadium.

I also received lots of fan mail: thousands of cards and letters. I remember when Pete Sheehy brought me my first batch of letters in a pillow case. I said, "What's this?" He said, "Your fan mail." Every Jewish mother in the world wanted to introduce me to her daughter, and each letter included a photograph. Jewish girls were writing to me, saying they wanted to come to the stadium to meet me.

My transformation, from naïve Jew to one conscious of his religion and its impact on others, was a speedy process. During my walks to and from the ballpark, I often stopped to eat at a delicatessen called the Roxy, which was right across the street from Manny's Baseball Land. I would usually enjoy the postgame spread at the stadium, but then have dessert at the Roxy. They had a delicious cheesecake, the sort of treat we were never given at the ballpark. Horace Clarke, my roommate, and I ate at the Roxy nearly every day when the Yankees were in town. The other customers of the Roxy were almost all Jews—little kids in *yarmulkes* and their parents—and they would read Jewish newspapers and magazines. I had never even *seen* a Jewish paper before arriving in the Bronx. Spending time at the Roxy opened my eyes, and I felt a major closeness to its patrons.

Trailblazers like Koufax shared their wisdom with me and impressed upon me the importance of taking my religion seriously. I met Koufax when he appeared at Yankee Stadium on Old Timers Day. I went up to introduce myself to him, but Sandy already knew who I was. He said he had followed my career because I was one of the few Jewish players in the big leagues. He reminded me to always wear my *chai* (a piece of Jewish jewelry that symbolizes "life") around my neck with respect—and that's exactly what I did.

I also met Greenberg, the best Jewish hitter of all time and the Jewish equivalent of Jackie Robinson. We spent a weekend together at Grossinger's, which was then a Jewish-owned Catskills resort in Liberty, New York. He talked to me about all of the anti-Semitic incidents he encountered during his playing days. During the 1930s, he was the only prominent Jewish player, and so he endured a lot of abuse from players, managers, and fans alike. People were upset and anxious during the Depression and needed to vent; Greenberg was an obvious target.

Riverdale, the portion of the Bronx where I lived, was 95 percent Jewish and was home to around 10 synagogues, from Reform to Conservative to Orthodox. It was an ideal area for me to live, and only strengthened my bond to the people of the city. If a young man from the South moved to New York City by himself, he would likely be overwhelmed and intimidated. But if he went to New York City as part of a family, he would feel comfortable. I felt like the whole city took me in—they were like family to me. Unlike my stay in the low minor leagues, I did not feel uneasy due to my religion.

The people of New York City were the greatest and most knowledgeable fans in the world. When I didn't have a good game, they booed. But when I did have a good game, they cheered even more loudly. I knew they loved me. They appreciated my efforts because I always gave my all when I stepped onto the ball field. When a player gives to the fans, they give back more. And that's what happened to me.

There was a teenage girl named Ursula who wore a replica of my No. 12 jersey to the games. She started a fan club for me, back before fan clubs were the norm. She always brought a bag of bagels for me and sat in right field, where I played early in my career. She carried a sign that read, "This is Boomer Territory." Similar signs soon appeared.

I was called "Boomer" by the writers and fans, and "Bloomie" by the players. Phil Rizzuto and Bill White hung the nickname "Boomer" on me after my first home run. First baseman George Scott, who played for Boston and Milwaukee in the late Sixties and Seventies, had the same nickname, and David

Wells later claimed it as well. But I was the New York Boomer, and to many I was also the Yiddish Yankee.

———————————

On one Sunday morning in 1973, I found out just how large my impact was on the city's Jewish population. I drove into the players' parking lot at Yankee Stadium at around eight in the morning. I knew we would have a full house that day because it was "Bat Day"—a popular giveaway at the gate—but I noticed an unusually large number of policemen and security people hanging around. As soon as I stepped out of the car, a policeman came over and said he needed to escort me into the stadium. There were a couple of hundred fans asking for autographs but the cops wouldn't let me sign for them.

I asked, "What's wrong? What's happening?" But they wouldn't explain the situation to me. I was escorted into the waiting room outside the Yankee offices, which were also full of security people. There, I was told that Rabbi Meir Kahane, the founder of the controversial Jewish Defense League, was coming to the game that day with a legion of his followers. I was aware of other Jewish organizations like the B'nai B'rith, but I knew little about the Jewish Defense League. I soon found out that it was a radical Jewish organization, considered by the FBI to be a terrorist group. The security personnel at Yankee Stadium were worried that the members might run out on the field and disrupt the game. They told me not to take batting practice for security reasons. I agreed, but mentioned that I was going to be playing right field that day.

They said they would put extra security people in that area of the stadium.

Prior to that day, I had always spoken with the fans out in right field—many of which were part of my fan club—before or during the game. But I was a little worried that day when I saw a lot of activity in the stands during the game's latter stages. There was a bit of a commotion among the fans in that area, and I saw one man in particular who was wearing a *yarmulke* causing a stir. But security put a stop to it. The members of the JDL in attendance were waving to the fans and yelling at me. I waved back.

A security guard sat on the bench with me during the entire game, but nothing ever happened. It turned out that the JDL wanted to present me with their "Jew of the Year" award. Eventually, I received their plaque: they gave it to somebody else to present to me. The Yankees would not allow them to present it in person. They wanted nothing to do with the group.

Being a Jewish Yankee was definitely a different experience than most of my teammates ever experienced. I received gifts from Israeli military leader Moshe Dayan and Israeli political leader Golda Meir. On one occasion, I even met Israeli Ambassador Simcha Dinitz, who used to attend a lot of Yankee games. The Ambassador said I had an open invitation from then-Prime Minister Meir to visit Israel as her guest. I felt honored by the gesture, which strengthened the kinship I felt for the Jewish people.

On the road, I often experienced a similar sense of belonging. Before a game in Boston, which also boasts a strong Jewish population, Red Sox general manager John Alezivos asked me to meet with a friend of his. Alezivos had been my minor-league general manager while I was with the Yankees' Manchester affiliate, and was also a college professor at Harvard. His friend entered the locker room wearing a *yarmulke*, and told me he was a rabbi. The rabbi said that I was a "chosen person" and that he felt like a chosen person, too, because he was in my presence. In many ways I did feel chosen. I attribute that feeling to my success in baseball despite my injuries, and to my becoming the first designated hitter.

Even before I met that rabbi, I had made it a point not to play on the High Holy Days. I never played on Rosh Hashanah or Yom Kippur. Growing up, I went to Kol Nidre services on Yom Kippur and stayed in the synagogue all day. I came home for an hour, then went back for the Yizkor service and stayed there. Then I broke the fast with my family.

Jewish holidays always begin at sundown. In 1973, we were playing a day game against the Cleveland Indians late in the season. Rosh Hashanah started at six o'clock that night. The game was tied with two outs in the bottom of the ninth inning, but we had a man on third base. I had to make a decision: quit the game for Rosh Hashanah or get a base hit. The Cleveland pitcher was a lefthander named Tom Hilgendorf who threw seeds. I got a clutch base hit to win the game—the biggest hit of my career. I cherish that at-bat more than anything else.

The game-winning hit made me a lot of new fans, too. I had told all the reporters that Rosh Hashanah was my holiday. And Ralph Houk supported me, saying that he would never stand between a player and his religion. I never had any trouble with any of my managers regarding my religion. The reporters jumped on the story—calling me the "Sundown Kid"—and from that day on, it felt like I was idolized by every Jew in New York City.

———————————————

The press really helped me to become accepted by fans in New York City. I owe a large debt to them. The team was struggling a lot early in my career, but the writers clung to me because I was energetic and talkative. They could come to me for a story about baseball, about eating, or about what I planned to do in the off-season. I think I was a novelty to them, in part because of my religion, but also in part due to the fact that unlike many other ballplayers, I always had a unique comment that would liven up a story. I answered their questions win or lose—even on days that I didn't play. They took care of me, and in turn I took care of them.

Most of my teammates ran away from the writers, but I embraced them, often hanging out with them away from the field. As a youth and even in my early years in the minors, I was always an extroverted person with a big following. Like Joe Namath or Magic Johnson, I just related to people so well. Plus, many of the writers were Jewish: Milton Richman, Vic Ziegel, Maury Allen, Murray Chass, and Moss Klein were all Jewish. I became real good friends with Bill Mazer, who had a sports talk show. We used to go out to dinner all the time.

But the writer I spent the most time with was Jim Ogle. Our friendship began when Jim wrote a big Sunday article for the Newark *Star-Ledger* about the different stages of my life. It was ironic in a way that I spent so much time with Jim, since he was a non-Jewish writer more than twice my age. We must have seemed like baseball's version of the Odd Couple. I was a young, fun-loving, Jewish guy from the South; Jim was a crusty guy in his late 60s, and an outcast from the sportswriting fraternity. He was seen as a "homer" amongst his peers, pushing the home team rather than producing objective articles. It didn't surprise anyone when he later went onto the Yankee payroll as the head of their Alumni Association.

Jim was far from a homer as far as I was concerned. He was like my father on the road. I even called him "Father Time." People thought I was sucking up to him, but he was a very nice person, and for some reason I could relate to him. Maybe it was because he was so easy to talk to. He treated me fairly—no differently than he treated any other Yankee player. When I had a bad game, he had a job to do and an accurate story to write.

I spent the most time with Jim, but I loved the press in general. When a reporter needed a quote, most of my teammates would head for the training room, where the press weren't allowed. But I sat there and gave them quotes. I made certain that I was available to the press. The way I looked at it, it was part of my obligation as a player.

The Yankees made every effort to market my religion for the team's benefit. It didn't matter to me; I was proud of my Jewish heritage. Thanks to the team's efforts—and my good relationship with the press—my popularity within the Jewish population continued to soar to new heights. I was a hit at every delicatessen in the city. I'd go to the Stage Deli and they would refuse to give me a check. The deli even named a sandwich after me: it was a big one, naturally, with corned beef, pastrami, and brisket. I was invited to Bar Mitzvahs, clinics in the Borscht Belt, synagogues, and countless speaking engagements on behalf of the B'nai B'rith and other organizations. I was contacted by every Jewish publication in the country. Rabbis would tell me that I was "part of the tribe."

I was a true celebrity. I appeared on the Jerry Lewis telethon, *The Ed Sullivan Show*, *The Tonight Show with Johnny Carson*, and *Good Morning America* when McLean Stephenson was the guest host and Alan Alda was also a guest. I had my likeness hung on the wall at a pair of famous restaurants: Elaine's and Sardi's. I was living a fantasy.

I always anticipated a downfall to my fame as a Jewish ballplayer, some sort of hatred spawned by anti-Semitic bigots. But such actions happened only once in a while. Although Hank Aaron received a hefty amount of hate mail as he was approaching Babe Ruth's home run record, I received only a handful of anti-Semitic letters. Every so often, a letter would arrive with no return address and a swastika or Ku Klux Klan sign inside. A few pieces of mail were addressed to "Jew-boy" or had a swastika on the envelope. I didn't even bother to open those. If they were death threats, I was better off not knowing about them. I tried never to engage someone who wished harm upon me. That's why I never got into an argument with the occasional loud-mouthed fan.

Through my stay in the south during the early portion of my minor-league career, I would occasionally hear abusive taunts from the crowd. I played ball in plenty of small coal mining or tobacco towns, and the townspeople looked at a Jew almost as an alien. In their eyes, I was quite different from them. In Winston-Salem, I hit a home run against Bill Lee, who later pitched for Boston. As I rounded the bases, I could hear someone shout from the stands, "Sit down, Jew-boy, you got horns!" I never looked up; I just touched home plate and returned to the dugout. I felt like I was above such fans and their actions.

Another memorable incident occurred while I was playing in Manchester, New Hampshire, which I thought was a very liberal, progressive town. I was good friends with a Jewish radio host from the town, so it came as quite a surprise when I had a bad experience in a local restaurant. I went into a seafood restaurant by myself, and the maitre d' sat me in the back of the place. I told him, "There are seats up front. I'd rather sit there." But he declined. When I asked him for his reasoning, he replied, "This was where I was instructed to put you so that you will get good service."

I could see what was going on. It was no secret that I was Jewish, as the press in Manchester had profiled me on several occasions. I recalled that I had often gone out to eat with black teammates in certain towns, and we were often placed in the back of the restaurant. But now I was in New England, and ordered to sit in the back, *by myself*. No one said a word about my religion—but they didn't have to. I received the message loud and clear.

There were other unpleasant incidents in the minors. But thankfully, things went a lot more smoothly in the majors.

Possibly, that was because people in bigger cities had more exposure to Jews and were more open-minded. In all the years I played in the majors, I never once heard a derogatory comment from a fan in the stands. Not even in Boston, where the fans were pretty hostile to the Yankees, or in Chicago, a big Polish town, or even in places where fans had too much to drink. They never said anything to me about being Jewish.

Too bad my teammates didn't react the same way: a couple of players were definitely anti-Semitic. I heard a couple of them refer to me as "The Jew" or say that New York City is "just a Jew city." They didn't dare say such a thing to a writer—only in talking among themselves. If I would have said something to the press about what I overheard, it would have become a big story. But I kept quiet because I respected my teammates as ballplayers. If they did not respect me as a Jew, that was their problem. I did not want to create any additional friction in the clubhouse.

Players were no different than fans: some were more educated and accepting than others. After the newspapers reported that I was going to observe Rosh Hashanah and Yom Kippur, a couple of my teammates weren't too happy about my decision. One of them came up to me and asked, "What are Rosh Hashanah and Yom Kippur?" I told him they were High Holy Days for Jewish people. He replied, "What are you? A Seventh-Day Adventist?" I told him I was Jewish and I intended to respect my beliefs. Too bad he couldn't do the same.

I guess some of my teammates were envious of me because I was receiving a lot of attention from the press. There was a good deal of animosity toward me. When I joined the team, it was centered around Bobby Murcer and Mel Stottlemyre. I could sense some of my teammates thinking, "Who is this kid getting all the attention? What's he ever done?" They were right, of course, but I didn't go *looking* for the attention; the writers came to me. They were nice to me, and I spent time with them, which was a no-no. Some thought I was cozying up to them, looking for publicity. But I just liked to talk, and the press came to me because I was talkative and gave them something to write about.

Despite my occasional popularity issues in the clubhouse, I was beginning to find additional demands on my time due to my popularity with fans. Elston Howard introduced me to Sheldon Stone, his agent and attorney, and we became the best of friends. Sheldon soon became my agent, manager, and attorney. He arranged bookings for me, and soon I was averaging three per weekend, though we once did as many as six. He had me traveling all over the place because there was a significant demand for me to appear at events.

I also did a few TV commercials and endorsed a few products for print advertisements. One of the biggest clients I worked with was the Hair Replacement Center. There was a clause in my contract that said I could not appear on TV or anywhere in public without wearing my hair weave, which was almost like a toupee but tied onto my head. It required a certain amount of upkeep and care, but I didn't always have the patience for that. One day I was doing a TV interview after a game and decided to take off the hair weave during a commercial break. It was a hot, humid night and it was itching really badly. After the break, I suddenly decided to take off my cap—forgetting that I had taken off the hair weave. The Hair Replacement Center saw the interview and went ballistic. I was their kingpin in New York. I had been in every magazine, from *Playboy* to *GQ*. Needless to say, that was the end of my contract. But there were others.

Everything I needed came free of charge. If I needed some shirts, I went down to the garment district, gave somebody a signed baseball or picture, and left with bags full of shirts and pants. I received meals "on the house" and rarely paid taxi fares. I was even waved through tollbooths. At that time, only the top players got commercials or enjoyed such perks, and I wasn't a top player. So some additional resentment built up among the players because of the opportunities I was receiving.

I was an easy target: I was the only Jewish player on the Yankees until Elliott Maddox came aboard in 1974. Then Ken Holtzman joined us in 1976. The first time I met Elliott, he was wearing a *chai* and said he was going to convert to Judaism. He was black, and so this news shocked me. I had never known anyone who converted to Judaism—let alone a black man who undoubtedly already had a good deal of discrimination to contend with. We talked about it and he said he believed in the faith. We became very close friends.

Holtzman was an introverted, intellectual guy who loved to read. When we acquired Kenny in June of 1976, I was excited. I was the first one to shake his hand when he joined the team. We became close friends as well. Later in life, Kenny became director of the Jewish Community Center in St. Louis.

Having supportive teammates to lean on helped me quickly forget any misguided discrimination I encountered from other teammates. But for the most part, I consider myself lucky to have been blessed to play with the men I did and to have played in New York City—among not only the best fans in the world, but the best *Jewish* fans, too.

6

A NEW "BOSS"

ittle did I know that fate had two major surprises in store
for both the Yankees and me in 1973: I became a designated hitter, and the team's ownership changed hands. George
Steinbrenner, a shipbuilder from Cleveland, formed a group and
purchased the club from CBS for $10 million, over $3 million
less than CBS had paid for the team. It turned out to be a tiny fee
in retrospect; *Forbes* listed the team's worth at an estimated $950
million in 2005.

CBS considered its ownership of the team a business deal—
it did not do a lot to improve the club. Then, in January of 1973,
I found out the Yankees were being sold to Steinbrenner's group.
After the first batting practice session of spring training, the new
owners were mingling around the field, introducing themselves
to everyone. Many of those within the group were Jewish and
made a point of introducing themselves to me and asking for my
autograph.

It soon became apparent that Steinbrenner was going to be much more of a hands-on owner. This wasn't just a corporate venture for him. There were slight bumps in pay, improvements to the weight room, and a new big-screen TV for the players. If anyone needed a couple of dozen bats, getting them was very simple. Under CBS, we always had to go upstairs to get approval. The corporate atmosphere disappeared in favor of a more family-oriented atmosphere.

When we won, we always received a letter of congratulations from one of the owners. George was around more and would come in and talk to us, even though he was commuting between Cleveland and New York at that time. He was very energetic and committed to improving the team's performance. He told the people who worked for him that the Yankees were going to field a winning team. His attitude was: "If you need something, you got it—don't worry about it."

The players received small bonuses, too, if we had a nice game. Once, after a long winning streak, we found an extra $400 cash in our lockers. Pete Sheehy would tell us, "You've got something underneath your glove." Those were the only bonuses Steinbrenner gave us, although Bill "Killer" Kane, the traveling secretary, would sometimes give us extra money for taxis. We had never seen such generosity before.

The team was glad that Steinbrenner took over. I loved him. To me, he was a wonderful human being. Sure, he was a hard-nosed type of guy, but any successful business required a successful leader—just like the military. We needed somebody we trusted and believed in. And if you gave George 100-percent effort, you could be assured of receiving 100 percent back.

Of course, George did have a temper, which has been well-documented. The first time I saw him become enraged was in 1976, the second year Catfish Hunter was with the team after coming over from Oakland as a free agent. I came to the stadium early with Thurman Munson, and Catfish was the only other player there. He always pitched with a wad of tobacco in his mouth, and some company wanted to do a tobacco commercial with him. They were filming the commercial, which was taking a long time, and Steinbrenner got mad because Catfish was pitching that day. It was an important game and Catfish didn't pitch well in it. Steinbrenner went absolutely berserk. I saw him jumping up and down outside his glass suite. After the game, Steinbrenner sent Catfish a letter of reprimand, and followed that up by yelling at Catfish in his office. Catfish returned red-faced and started cussing in his southern drawl. He said, "This guy is just like Finley," referring to A's owner Charley Finley.

Steinbrenner's passion for the game—and winning—was second to none. Money was no object to him; as he's since shown time and time again, he'll spend as much as necessary to win. But in the process of spending, George often stepped on the toes of his managers and general managers, insisting on trades or free-agent signings they didn't approve of and often conducting the negotiations himself. Steinbrenner's dominance over the decision-making within the Yankees franchise wasn't limited to the front office. One of the original partners in his ownership group, John McMullen, once said that nothing was more limited than being a limited partner of George Steinbrenner.

Patience was not one of Steinbrenner's virtues. Although he later found some stability under manager Joe Torre, George often changed managers, players, pitching coaches, and public relations directors—firing, trading, or releasing them for minor offenses but often bringing them back for second or third stints. He had a love-hate relationship with Billy Martin, whom he hired as manager five times—a major-league record. The New York press dubbed him "The Boss" with good reason. He was visible, vocal, and controversial. He would even call the manager in the dugout during games to offer suggestions. Most importantly, he was *in charge.*

It didn't surprise me when Steinbrenner got into trouble with the commissioner of baseball in 1974. Bowie Kuhn suspended him for two years after he pleaded guilty to a felony involving an illegal contribution to the 1972 presidential campaign of Richard M. Nixon. He was reinstated early—just in time for the start of spring training games in 1976.

From my perspective, George was guilty of only one thing: wanting to win at all costs. When he bought the team, he told us he would do whatever it took to win. His word was good. The 1973 team that Steinbrenner inherited wasn't a great team. In '73, Munson, Bobby Murcer, and Graig Nettles all hit more than 20 home runs, Mel Stottlemyre and Doc Medich were solid starters, and Sparky Lyle recorded 27 saves. But there wasn't much else to work with. Of course, I enjoyed some fame as the league's first designated hitter and posted the best average of my career at .329. But Jim Ray Hart, a veteran righthanded slugger acquired from San Francisco early in the '73 season, wound up as the primary designated hitter. His 106 games as the DH were nearly double my total of 56.

Ralph Houk, in his second stint as Yankee manager, realized the team was not even close in terms of talent to the championship-caliber teams he managed in 1961, '62, and '63. After the '73 Yankees limped to a fourth-place finish, The Major, as we called Houk, resigned. Unhappy with the new front office in New York, he turned up as manager of the Detroit Tigers the following season. Lee MacPhail left, too. His main contribution as general manager had been trading Danny Cater to Boston for Sparky Lyle—a deal that convinced the Red Sox never to trade with the Yankees again.

The '73 season was also the last for Mike Burke, who was team president during the CBS days. He had been part of Steinbrenner's ownership group, but didn't command the same authority under The Boss. Gabe Paul, another of Steinbrenner's cronies from Cleveland, took over as team president and immediately tried to make his mark by hiring manager Dick Williams away from the Oakland A's. Williams was coming off consecutive world championships with the A's, and Oakland owner Charley Finley demanded a player as compensation. Paul refused and signed Williams anyway, but then lost him when league president Joe Cronin upheld Finley's protest. Williams went on to find employment with the Angels, and Paul continued his search.

Bill Virdon, a straight-laced guy who had managed the Pittsburgh Pirates for a couple of years, was Paul's second choice for the open managerial position. The Yankees were happy to have him. Virdon had spent four years in the Yankees' minor-league system in the early Fifties as the major league team's outfield was loaded—Gene Woodling, Hank Bauer, Irv Noren, and a young Mickey Mantle competed for playing time in the outfield at that time. So Virdon was dealt to the Cardinals for 38-year-old Enos Slaughter. In 1955, Virdon was named Rookie of the Year in the National League, and the following season he was dealt to the Pirates, where he became a Gold Glove centerfielder during his ten seasons with the team.

Virdon managed in the minors before returning to the Pirates as a coach and then manager. In his first year as skipper in 1972, the Pirates won the NL East title but lost in the playoffs to Cincinnati. When Pittsburgh struggled in 1973, Virdon lost his job in September but wasn't unemployed long, as the Yankees soon came calling. Virdon would become the only Yankee manager to never win a game in Yankee Stadium: the Bronx ballpark was undergoing major renovations in 1974 and 1975, and during that time the Yankees played their home games at Shea Stadium. By 1976, when the Yankees were set to play ball at Yankee Stadium once again, Virdon was out as manager.

We spent our second year under Steinbrenner away at Shea, as tenants of the New York Mets. We were excited about the renovations going on at Yankee Stadium, but we felt like step-children at Shea. The home of the Mets was built on a landfill. It was a swamp: cold, windy, and smelly—on the field and in the clubhouse. So as not to interfere with the Mets, we did not use their clubhouse. We used the locker room of the New York Jets football team, and the team's offices were located in a building on the grounds of the World's Fair, across the highway from Shea. We could tell early on that life at Shea was going to be no picnic. On our first day working out there, the field was rough and the noise from jets flying overhead was a nuisance. But at least we were still in New York City.

The transition from Houk to Virdon was a bit of a shock. Virdon didn't take any crap from anybody. When he had something to get off his chest, he knew how to get the team's attention. He didn't talk much, but when he did people listened. He placed more restrictions on the team than Ralph did, but regardless of his managerial style, I thought he was an excellent leader. We called him Popeye because he had such large forearms. He always wore a short-sleeved shirt to show off what good shape he was in. And he wanted his players in good shape, too. Bill's workouts were tough. He ordered daily base-running drills that were so demanding that some of the guys complained that it was as if they were in boot camp. Having experienced boot camp, I knew better. But Virdon did run a tight ship.

All that discipline might have worked to our advantage if not for the uncomfortable environment we were playing in. Shea Stadium was a lousy place to hit—especially for lefthanded hitters who were used to the short porch at Yankee Stadium. The ball simply didn't travel there, making it difficult to hit home runs. I hit a pair in a day-night doubleheader against the Texas Rangers early in the 1974 season, but most of my home runs—nine out of 14—came on the road during the two years we played at Shea. On the road that year, I hit three homers in a doubleheader against the Cleveland Indians late in the season.

Bobby Murcer really suffered in the stadium transition. After hitting 22 homers in 1973, he hit just 10 in '74—including only two at Shea. Then he broke his thumb trying to break up a hotel fight between Rick Dempsey and Bill Sudakis. In addition to losing Murcer when we needed him most, Mel Stottlemyre's career ended at age 32 because of a shoulder injury.

But we still gave the Orioles a run for their money. Graig Nettles was our top home run hitter with 22, Lou Piniella and Elliott Maddox both topped .300 in batting average, and Thurman Munson became a real leader in the clubhouse. Sudakis was a great jack-of-all-trades, and Gene "Stick" Michael was a slick fielder at three infield positions. I led the team with a .311 average, and hit 10 homers in limited playing time. I'm sure I would have hit a lot more if I had been healthy, but I had problems with my hamstrings and my shoulder.

Chris Chambliss and Sandy Alomar were brought on board during the season to tighten up the right side of our infield. That helped our pitching staff, led by a pair of 19-game winners, Doc Medich and Pat Dobson, with Sparky Lyle in relief. The injuries to Stottlemyre and Rudy May really hurt our chances.

We had a two-and-a-half-game lead over Baltimore in mid-September, but then lost three straight to the Orioles in New York. That gave the O's the momentum they needed to win the division by two games. Down the stretch, they won close games, one after the other, finishing the season on a 28-6 streak. Baltimore's pitching was just too good. Although Jim Palmer had a sore arm that knocked him out as the staff ace, the Orioles received top seasons from three lefties: Mike Cuellar, Ross Grimsley, and Dave McNally. The trio won 56 games that year.

Though we didn't have a championship team, we drew pretty good crowds. A lot of Mets fans came to the Yankee games, so we had a blending of Mets and Yankees fans. I'm sure we would have won more games if we had stayed at Yankee Stadium, but the team made a big jump in the standings anyway during our first year in Flushing.

––––––––––––––––––

Following the 1974 season, it was time to ask for a raise. Negotiating a contract with Gabe Paul was a long process, requiring lots of meetings and back and forth. Feeling pretty good about my chances, I went to see him, accompanied by my agent Sheldon Stone. I was coming off a decent year, and I started the conversation by saying, "Why don't you trade me?" Paul replied, "No team will want you." Then he laughed and said, "We'll never trade you. You're the token on this team."

He meant—the Jewish player. Not many people know this, but Paul was Jewish, too. It was a secret in baseball. Due to his religion, he felt a connection to Sheldon and me and often joked with us. He also looked out for me, making recommendations on my behalf.

But when it came to business, he wouldn't kid around. Before the start of free agency, everybody had one-year contracts. Paul treated me the same as everyone else: he would send out a contract that he knew was unsatisfactory and would be rejected. That would get the ball rolling. Sheldon would pick me up in Riverdale, we'd drive to Paul's office, and ask ourselves along the way, "What do you think he's going to say today?" Once we arrived, Paul would proceed tell me how bad I had been the previous year. Anything good that I had accomplished was discarded. He had statistics and charts to show each player how much of a liability he was to the team. It was obviously a ploy to keep the payroll as low as possible. Paul would counter our demands with a new lowball offer, we'd reject it, and then make another counteroffer. Then he would say he wanted to think about it. He knew the figure we were going to sign for all along, but we still had to go through the process.

We'd be asking for a raise of $200 a month, but he'd offer a $25 or $50 raise instead. He would say, "Let me think about this. Let me look at everything. Come back in 10 days and we'll talk again." We'd come back and he would increase his offer to $115 a month. We still wanted $200. He'd say, "I have to think about that" and make us come back. It was incredible. I think he just enjoyed our company.

I got so exasperated with him on one occasion that I said, "If you make another comment like that, I'm going to pick you up and throw you out the window." He laughed and said, "Why don't you show this kind of spunk on the baseball field?" I said, "I do. Why do you think I hit over .300?"

In the mid-Seventies, Paul brought Tal Smith into the negotiating sessions. Smith was a young executive who had just joined the Yankees from Houston. Paul would say to Smith: "What do you think, Tal? Should we give him a raise or a cut? He didn't get a hit on [such-and-such a day]."

When Paul left the Yankees a few years later, he was replaced by another Jewish man, Al Rosen, who was one of Steinbrenner's friends. But before he left following the 1977 season, Paul managed to put together a team that would win the World Series.

I enjoyed my first taste of a pennant race in '74, and the Yankees expected big things the following year. Steinbrenner made a big splash when he signed Catfish Hunter, who had won 106 games over the previous five seasons, and won another 23 for us in '75. Hunter had stumbled upon a loophole that freed him from his contract with Oakland. The team also traded Bobby Murcer to San Francisco for Bobby Bonds. The Yankees wanted more speed in the lineup, but also another righthanded hitter to make their attack more balanced. Bonds filled both needs, clubbing 32 homers and swiping 30 bases for us that season. That made Bonds the first 30-30 player in Yankee history.

The writers suggested another reason for the Murcer trade was because I was ready to supply a lot of the lefthanded power we lost when Murcer was dealt. But I failed: Once again I suffered all kinds of physical problems during the '75 season and hit only .255, by far the worst of my career, with only four home runs. I was limited to just 34 games and 106 at-bats. I didn't know it at the time, but my home run on July 8 against the Rangers' Steve Hargan would be my last as a Yankee. Piniella also missed a good portion of the season as well, and despite solid seasons from Chambliss, Maddox, Munson, Nettles, and Roy White, the Yankees missed our bats.

To make matters worse, Bill Virdon lost his job in early August. Steinbrenner brought in Billy Martin, who had started that season as manager of the Texas Rangers. To say that Billy was brash would be the understatement of the century. He was a lit-

tle guy with a big mouth, and he got into all kinds of battles—
with fans, writers, owners, and even his own players. Off the
field, his barroom fights became the stuff of legend. He was an
enigma to many people because he could manage a ballclub better than he could manage himself.

Billy had been a pretty solid second baseman for the Yankees
in the Fifties, even winning a World Series MVP
award in 1953. During his playing days, he hung out with Mickey
Mantle and Whitey Ford—until the Yankees traded
him away after he got into a fight at the Copacabana night club.
Before he returned to the Yankees as field manager, Billy's teams
took divisional titles with the Minnesota Twins and Detroit
Tigers, and he transformed the Rangers from perennial losers
into division contenders in just one season. But Billy never
enjoyed a lengthy tenure. Controversy clung to him like a shad-
ow.

Still, George Steinbrenner was willing to take his chances.
Even though Virdon had a winning record at the time he was
fired—the Yankees were 53-51—George grew interested in
Billy the minute the Rangers let him go that summer. Martin's
magic didn't take effect right away. To finish out the season,
the Yankees improved only marginally and ended in third place,
12 games behind the Boston Red Sox and seven and a half behind
second-place Baltimore. Considering his reputation, Billy was
uncharacteristically quiet during his first few months as Yankee
manager. Maybe he was getting his feet wet under Steinbrenner.
But George was pretty quiet, too. The classic Billy-George con-
frontations would come later.

7
SHOULDERING
THE SUPERSTAR
LABEL

hen I was taken with the top pick in the 1967 draft, everyone told me that I had superstar potential. Scouts said they had never seen somebody with my combination of strength, speed, and fundamentals. I was considered a "five-tool prospect," a tag scouts and writers use to describe a player who hits for both power and average, runs the bases well, fields his position with ease, and possesses a strong throwing arm. But the thing they didn't tell me was that I would have to overcome career-threatening injuries. As my career progressed, the DL—disabled list—became as big of a negative for me as the DH—designated hitter—was a positive.

I couldn't help the injuries. I was a big, strong kid—6 foot 2 and 205 pounds—and I gave 100 percent every time I stepped on the field. I didn't know how to not play hard. And unfortunately, I was just the type of player who was susceptible to injuries. Hamstring pulls became commonplace for me, and while I tried to play through them, they diminished my speed. In an effort to deter the hamstring problems, the Yankees actually sent me to do stretching exercises with the New York City Ballet. They had me stretching with dancers, hoping to increase my flexibility, which was poor. I was never able to touch my toes.

During my first three seasons, a series of nagging injuries limited my playing time. But I still managed to play through the pain. I never complained; in fact, I hoped that I would see *more* playing time. Then I endured my first serious setback on the final day of the 1974 season. In the first inning of a game against the Brewers, I hit a long home run off Jim Colborn. In the process of swinging, I ripped my right shoulder during the follow-through of my swing and collapsed at home plate in pain. Gene Monahan, our trainer, raced out with his assistant, Herman Schneider. They looked at my shoulder but weren't quite sure what to make of it. I finally got up and ran around the bases. I stayed in the game until the bottom of the ninth, when I was lifted for a defensive replacement.

After the game, my shoulder and arm were limp. The doctor came in to look at my shoulder, but an accurate prognosis couldn't be determined. The doctor felt around and decided that I had sprained it. He told me to ice down my shoulder, and predicted that I'd be pain-free in a few days. I took his advice, but when I woke up the next morning I had very severe bruising—I was all black and blue. I had no strength whatsoever. Team doctor Sidney Gaynor looked at the shoulder and said I was okay. But I told him I couldn't move my arm and I was in a heap of pain. Dr. Gaynor instructed me to continue to use ice and heat to treat the injury. With time—a good deal of it spent in the whirlpool—he thought that my condition would improve. Monahan worked on me for three or four hours, but the shoulder still caused me significant pain. I tried to pick up a bat and couldn't even do that.

The doctors thought I was suffering from a muscle or tendon problem that would heal on its own. They put me in a leather harness and tried other treatments to avoid having to operate on my shoulder. At that time, major reconstructive surgeries were still a mystery. Dr. Frank Jobe completed his first elbow tendon surgery on Dodgers pitcher Tommy John in 1974. It would be 18 months before anyone knew whether the surgery would be a success, however. It was a stunning success, and so Jobe's "Tommy John" surgery—as it was called from that day on—became a common operation in baseball. My problem was that I needed rotator cuff surgery. My tendon was torn, and it was not going to heal on its own. Rotator cuff surgeries also eventually became a normal procedure in sports, but at that time they were not.

Even after a full off-season of rest, my shoulder still wasn't right in 1975. I tried to play through the pain, but my performance on the field reflected my injuries; I posted the lowest batting average of my career. After the season, the Yankees ordered me to try to rebuild my strength using Nautilus machines—something new at that time. I became quite muscular, but the weight training wasn't healing my tendon, and my shoulder still bothered me. In spring training the following year, I was still suffering through shoulder pain. Whenever I pressed on my shoulder, there was a sharp pain.

continued on page 90

Welcome to the big leagues kid: Mickey Mantle gives the newcomers
a few pointers in 1969. Left to right: Jim Lyttle, Rusty Torres,
Mickey Mantle, and me. *Photograph by Michael Grossbardt.*

I was all smiles my first few seasons with the Yankees.
National Baseball Hall of Fame Library, Cooperstown, N.Y.

There goes a two-run homer off the Twins' Jim Perry in July of 1972.
Louis Requena/MLB Photos via Getty Images

In 1973 and '74, I posted two straight seasons with a .300-plus average. It felt good to begin to live up to the hype of being "the next Mickey Mantle." *National Baseball Hall of Fame Library, Cooperstown, N.Y.*

I earned a lot of notoriety as baseball's first designated hitter, including a display at the National Baseball Hall of Fame.
National Baseball Hall of Fame Library, Cooperstown, N.Y.

My mother, Goldie Rae, and father, Sol, help me celebrate the birth of my son, Adam, in 1976. Adam sports his dad's jersey number, 12.
Courtesy of Mara Young

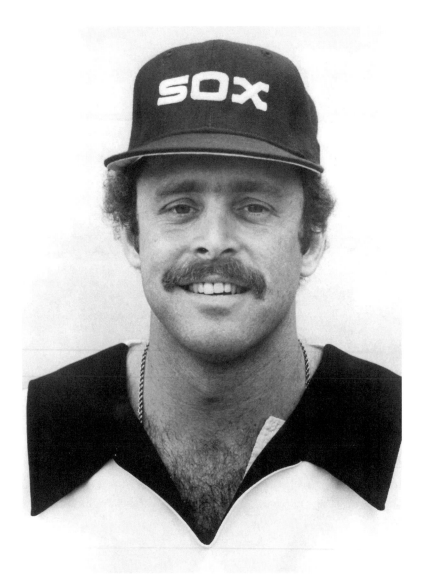

As a free agent following the 1977 season, I tried to turn over a new leaf with Bill Veeck's Chicago White Sox.
National Baseball Hall of Fame Library, Cooperstown, N.Y.

Hanging out in Chicago with my son, Adam, and my good friend and agent, Sheldon Stone. *Courtesy of Mara Young*

Adam probably got me interested in becoming a hitting instructor for kids during his stint in T-ball in 1983. *Courtesy of Mara Young*

My daughter Chesley and I on the day of her senior prom in 2004.
Courtesy of Ron Blomberg

My family means the world to me. Left to right: my daughter, Chesley; me; my son's fiancé, Adrianne; my son, Adam; and my wife, Beth. *Courtesy of Mara Young*

I suppose you're never too old to "call your shot." Here I am at the annual Old Timers Day game at Yankee Stadium in 2005.
Diamond Images/Getty Images

continued from page 77

This time, however, I kept quiet about the injury. After spending two years at Shea Stadium, I was anxious to play in the new-and-improved Yankee Stadium. I liked that short right field porch, and I was glad they changed the distance to Death Valley, in left center, from 457 to 430 feet. I was so strong from the weight training that I could whip my wrists to drive the ball. But that was not my natural strength that I displayed prior to the injury. I just could not produce the power I was accustomed to. I once hit a ball off the top of the Yankee Stadium facade in batting practice. Mickey Mantle was the only other guy who came close to hitting the ball out of the ballpark. His smacked into the facade but mine hit higher up, right at the top. If it wasn't for the facade, it would have left the stadium. No one had ever seen a ball hit that far. Tony Ferrara, who threw batting practice for the team for 25 years, said that was the longest home run he had ever witnessed.

But I didn't know if that power would ever return. I knew deep down that something was wrong with my shoulder. I couldn't throw hard and I was afraid to take a full swing. My performance on the field spoke for itself. With my power zapped, I was reduced to a singles hitter. Finally, George Steinbrenner called me up to his office and said, " Bloomie, we need you. You've got to play." And I said, " George, my shoulder is so bad. Something is wrong with it." He said Dr. Gaynor reported that my shoulder was strained. They gave me a muscle stress test, and took X-rays on the shoulder. But X-rays would only show whether something was broken, not if a tendon was torn. To complicate matters, I was noticeably muscular and had the appearance of being quite strong, thanks to my work on the Nautilus machines. I looked rock solid, but the problem lay underneath the surface.

"George," I said, "when I'm in the cage and see an inside pitch, I can't let my swing go. It's really bad."

This angered Steinbrenner: "Bloomie," he said, "we're paying you a lot of money. We need you right now, and I'm hurt by this. You're one of our best hitters. You're a superstar. You need to play."

I headed downstairs and went straight to Billy Martin, telling him, "I'm here early. I want to take batting practice. I want to play." This was the first time in my career I saw some of my teammates obviously give me the cold shoulder. They thought I was faking my injury. Somebody told a writer that the team needed me badly. The person told the press that I was at the ballpark every day taking batting practice and thought that I could play. I was so frustrated—upset that I wouldn't heal, disappointed that my teammates thought I wasn't being honest, and sad that they had lost faith in me. It killed me more than anything else I've ever gone through in my life.

I had always been an athlete who loved to play the game. I wanted to play every day, which is why I was so frustrated that I had become a platoon hitter. But what could I do in this situation? It was a lose-lose proposition for me. The team doctor thought I could play and so the team wanted me to play, but I was in such pain and my performance had dropped off severely. I couldn't meet the team's expectations. More tests were done, and I was given a shot to curb the pain. The shots helped out a little bit, but the results were not long-lasting. I thought I needed surgery, and in the end I turned out to be right.

A week before we broke camp, we played a night game against the Minnesota Twins. I was facing Mark Wiley, a pitcher who was attempting to preserve his major league career. I took a huge swing, just let it go, and the pain immediately shot through my shoulder. I fell down and began to see stars. The trainers came running out of the dugout and I went straight to the training table. I'll never forget what Martin said to me: "You really let me down. It's a week before the season starts. You're hitting .300 and everybody thought you were back. You were out for a long time last year. Now you're on the shelf again." He wasn't finished. "We relied on you," he told me. "We released players because of you. We wanted to play you every day. Now we have no designated hitter." Billy was red as fire. The veins in his neck were sticking out. The Yankees had brought Tommy Davis, twice a National League batting champ, to spring training for a trial as a righthanded DH. But the team let him go shortly before that incident. I was supposed to be the main guy, but my shoulder wouldn't cooperate.

Danny Kannel, a team doctor, finally made a sensible recommendation, asking the team to send me to California to see Dr. Robert Kerlan and Dr. Frank Jobe, both experts when it came to elbows and shoulders. At age 27, I should have been in the prime of my career. Instead, I was headed to Los Angeles with the prospects of surgery and a long rehabiliation.

Doctors Jobe and Kerlan injected dye into my shoulder, performed all sorts of tests, and finally decided that I was suffering from severe tendinitis. My bicep was completely torn away, but because I was so big and strong, it was hard to see the injury. They said, "No wonder you can't hit or throw a baseball. You don't have a tendon."

Two days later, I went through a reconstructive operation. All of a sudden, I received flowers and phone calls from Steinbrenner and Gabe Paul, and I felt like part of the team again. But it would be a while before I could play; the doctors told me I would need a good eight to ten months of rehabilitation. They also said that the tendon had actually snapped at the point where it went directly over my shoulder. They tied the tendon back to the humerus bone rather than bring it over my shoulder again. They said I would never have 100 percent mobility in that arm, but that with rehab I could be at 60-70 percent. That would allow me to swing a bat and throw decently—but not from the outfield. My time in the future would have to be spent at first base or as a DH.

I spent about a month in California at Centralia Hospital, which housed all the stars and athletes. Walter Matthau, the comedian, was in the room right next to me. When I finally returned to Yankee Stadium a little over a month after my surgery, I spent time doing exercises to strengthen my shoulder. But I never lifted a bat.

Billy Martin was somewhat kinder to me, but some of my teammates weren't. All of a sudden, harrowing signs would appear: "Blomberg's Whirlpool" or "Blomberg's Training Table." It was a little bit of a dig, and it made me feel like an outcast on my own team. I dreaded going to the stadium I was once so excited to return to because it was hard to face the guys. I was going through my rehab while they were taking batting practice; I was leaving when they were coming in. I listened to the games on the radio, but I felt like a hanger-on. Sometimes I stayed at the park to watch the games, but I sat up in the press box with the writers instead of in the dugout with my teammates.

I just felt awful, physically and emotionally. But the Jewish fans were still supporting me. Wherever I went in public, they still clung to me. They told me they prayed for my shoulder to heal. Still, I felt like a player without a team. The only distraction was rehab. I worked hard to come back from my shoulder injury. Sports medicine was different then. Today, they could scope my shoulder—a simple procedure—and I'd be good as new in no time. In 1976, the only way that injury could be repaired was by cutting open the shoulder. That meant six months of rehabilitation time.

Late in the '76 season, the team was doing well and I was hitting well in batting practice. So the Yankees activated me at the end of the season. I came into the on-deck circle at Yankee Stadium before a packed house. The whole stadium stood and applauded, chanting, "Boomer! Boomer!" for a minute or two. I grounded out and they all stood up again. That was one of the best receptions I ever enjoyed. I felt as if I were coming back to life. It took me eight months of working my stinking tail off— lifting weights, stretching, and running—but I was finally back. And it was great that the fans still appreciated me.

When the Yankees made it to the World Series that year, it absolutely killed me not to be able to play. I was on the field for introductions and in the dugout before the game, but then I had to leave the dugout during the game. Only players who were on the active roster were allowed to be in the dugout during the game. Watching my team finally succeed while I struggled was difficult. Until I hurt my shoulder in 1974, my career was going strong. Then, all of a sudden, I hit a wall. Emotionally, I wasn't able to handle it well. That '76 team had a certain unity, and I was not a part of it. Thurman Munson, Roy White, and Willie Randolph were all great to me, but there were a few guys who thought I was injury-prone and was never going to make a successful comeback. They thought I was taking someone's money—maybe theirs. So that made for plenty of tense times.

But at least the team did well. In his first season with the club after arriving from the Angels, Mickey Rivers proved to be the perfect lead-off hitter, hitting well over .300 and stealing more than 40 bases. Randolph, a 21-year-old second baseman obtained from the Pittsburgh organization, also thrived in his first year, becoming a great No. 2 hitter. Graig Nettles gave us Gold Glove defense at third base and hit 32 home runs, tops in the league. The team quarterback—our leader—was Munson, who won the first Most Valuable Player award by a Yankee since Elston Howard in 1963. He also became the first Yankee to be named captain since Lou Gehrig 50 years earlier.

Lou Piniella provided several big hits that season but gave the team its biggest lift on May 20 against the Red Sox. He slid hard into Boston catcher Carlton Fisk on a play at the plate, knocking Fisk over with a football-like tackle. Both benches emptied and a brawl ensued. Red Sox Bill Lee and Luis Tiant started punching members of the Yankees. Rico Petrocelli and

Carl Yastrzemski joined the fray, and Nettles and I were involved from our side. Piniella was called out on the play, but the Yankees played a lot better after the brawl and ran away with the division.

Our pitching helped. Ed Figueroa and Dock Ellis, both acquired by Gabe Paul in trades, teamed with Catfish Hunter to give the Yankees three top starters with 53 wins on the season between them. Meanwhile, Sparky Lyle led the league in saves, anchoring an effective pen that included Dick Tidrow and Grant Jackson.

We wouldn't have reached the World Series without Chris Chambliss. There was no Division Series then, just a best-of-five League Championship Series. Chris hit over .500 with two home runs and eight RBI in the series, but the one hit that meant the most came in the ninth inning of Game 5. With the Yankees tied with the Royals 6-6, Chambliss crushed a homer over the center-field fence against Mark Littell to give New York the victory. Yankee fans went wild, pouring onto the field, and I'm not sure Chris made it all the way around the bases. It was the most dramatic finish I had ever seen.

Unfortunately, the momentum didn't last. The World Series against Cincinnati—who swept us in four games— proved to be forgettable except for one thing: Dan Driessen of the Reds became the first designated hitter in World Series history. Before 1976, the DH was never used in games involving National League teams, but Commissioner Bowie Kuhn broke a deadlock between leagues when he voted to allow it in the World Series. At first, it was used in alternating years, but later it was allowed in all games played in American League parks.

Like me, Driessen was a young, power-hitting first baseman who became a DH out of necessity: the Reds had Tony
Perez, a future Hall of Famer, at first base. Had I been healthy, I
might have been the first World Series DH. The Series opened
in Riverfront Stadium, so the Yankees batted first in the game,
which might have given me the opportunity to earn a second
distinction related to the DH rule. But it was not to be. I could-
n't parlay two September at-bats into a World Series roster spot.
All I could do was hope that I'd feel okay the following season,
and be able to get my career back on track.

I was looking forward to the 1977 season. The surgery had
repaired my shoulder, the Yankees were defending American
League champions, and we had signed the best free agent on the
market: Reggie Jackson. I had worked my whole life to be a part
of the Yankees' success, and so the '76 season was a real disap-
pointment for me. I desperately wanted to be a part of the
Yankees winning tradition. Instead, I was forced to be a spectator rather than a participant.

Everything should have been rosy in 1977. I thought I had
a new contract on life as a ballplayer—with my injuries finally
behind me. But right off the bat, a telling tone was set. When I
reported to spring training in Fort Lauderdale, Billy Martin
wouldn't speak to me. Many of my teammates wouldn't speak
to me, either. Only a few teammates—Thurman Munson, Ron
Guidry, Goose Gossage, and Lou Piniella—and some of the
coaches—especially Dick Howser and Elston Howard—were

good to me. But Billy treated me like I was a ghost. He would walk right past me. That old familiar tension resurfaced in the clubhouse. Now that I wasn't considered a superstar-in-the-wings, some anti-Semitism emerged on occasion from a few of my teammates.

Once the exhibition games started that spring, I had plenty of at-bats and hit the ball well. I was hitting home runs, even hitting the light towers in Little Yankee Stadium, our nickname for the stadium in Fort Lauderdale. I was like a kid again. Then, for some unknown reason, Martin decided to put me in left field. Maybe he put me there deliberately so I would embarrass myself. I think he was still miffed that I hadn't told him about my bad shoulder sooner in 1976. I had played a lot of right field early in my career, but left field was a strange position for me. And I hadn't played the outfield *at all* in four years.

We were playing a game in Chain O' Lakes Park in Winter Haven, Florida, where the outfield was surrounded by a concrete wall with no padding. Gary Carter had run into the same wall the previous year and it took 40 stitches to sew him back up. Early in the game, Carl Yastrzemski—a left-handed batter—sliced the ball to the opposite field, in my general direction. I took off after it and ran full-blast into the wall. I was knocked out cold, and Yaz got an inside-the-park home run.

My teammates thought I was dead. They said that was the hardest they had ever seen anybody hit a wall. Since Yastrzemski was a lefthanded hitter, I was playing him to slice the ball. But he hit it pretty well and there was a halfway-decent wind blowing that day. So it took a lot of effort just to reach the ball. And before I could, I smacked right into the wall, ramming my left knee directly into it.

I was out cold. When I finally looked up, Billy Martin, all the coaches, and Herm Schneider were standing over me. I was covered in blood. I couldn't move my knee and I had a big gash in the center of it. Blood was gushing out of the gash, and bones were sticking out. There was glass all over my face where my sunglasses had dug into my nose. It was a gruesome sight, and I had to be carted off the field since I couldn't walk. They fixed me up temporarily in the locker room, and then—still in my uniform—I was taken to the bus so that I could make the five-hour trip from Winter Haven back to Fort Lauderdale. On the bus, my leg was propped up in the air, and trainer Herm Schneider doled out the pain medication. Dr. Danny Kannel, an orthopedist who worked for the Yankees, looked at my knee and said I had shattered my knee cap and torn up all the cartilage inside. Just looking at it, his diagnosis sounded about right.

After missing almost all of the 1976 season and feeling isolated from the team, I had big hopes for 1977. When I blew out my left knee, I felt like a jinxed man. It was déjà vu. As bad as the '76 season had been for me, the '77 season would be even worse. The most frustrating aspect of the season was that the writers—who I had befriended upon my arrival and remained friends with through my career—kept asking me how I was doing. Was I making progress in my rehabilitation? When did I expect to be back? To no one's surprise, even though I hadn't contributed in two seasons and was injured again, my name was still popping up in the newspaper and it angered two or three guys on the team. And they were vocal about it. When team publicist Bob Fishel walked into the clubhouse without limping after his own knee surgery, somebody said, "At least Fishel's ready to play even if Blomberg isn't."

One of our top stars went public, telling a newspaper reporter, "How in the world can [Blomberg] come into the clubhouse and let people interview him when he's been out of baseball for a year? He should be playing. I don't know if he's injured or not. We're carrying this guy. We need him. But we don't feel like he's part of the team anymore. All he does is come to the clubhouse, talk to the reporters, and go up in the press box. He gets all this publicity for doing nothing. *And he gets paid for it!*"

I went nuts when I read it. I went to the ballpark to confront him, waiting two hours for him to show up. I confronted him right outside the tunnel, asking him, "How can you say this about me?" He told me just what he said to the writer: "You're down here doing nothing." I was livid, but my cooler head prevailed and I decided not to be a jerk about it. I walked away, but I felt better because I had at least aired my frustration.

He was actually right about my routine: I would come in for treatments, then go up to the press box and sit with Herb Clark and Seymour Siwoff. The fans always waved to me and offered their encouragement when I sat up there, and that killed me every time. I left games early—often in the second or third inning. The support of those fans meant everything to me, since I was suffering from depression. Fans gravitated toward me because I was nice to them. I signed autographs, talked to them, and even sat down to have lunch with them. The fan support was wonderful, and was one of the main factors that helped me keep my sanity those two seasons I spent on the disabled list.

Most of the writers supported me too. But there was one notable exception: Henry Hecht of *The New York Post*. Hecht took the side of some of my teammates, agreeing with those who said that I was a distraction who wasn't contributing to the team. He rarely had anything good to say about me; he was constantly derogatory toward me. When I was down, he pushed me further down. Considering that he was a Jewish writer, I thought that he might be in my corner. But he was not, and so he was the only writer I tried to avoid.

The 1977 season was not just a difficult time in my career, but also in my life. I met with a psychiatrist once a week for about four or five weeks. It was the team's idea, but I agreed to do it. I had been an extrovert my whole life, but in 1977 I went into a shell as my world came crashing down around me when I realized that I was not going to live up to my potential as a player. I felt that I let the team, the fans, and myself down. I lost confidence in myself. For nine seasons of professional ball, I was used to going to the ballpark and seeing my name on the lineup card. When it wasn't, I would sit on the bench, waiting for a chance to pinch-hit. But for those two seasons, the only time I saw my name, it was followed by the words, "INACTIVE. DISABLED LIST."

I was at the lowest point of my career, and I felt totally alone. I tried to stay out of the public eye as often as possible, and I would not answer the telephone. For once, I wanted to avoid people, because everyone wanted to ask the same questions: When was I going to be back in the lineup? I didn't have any idea, and that truth scared me. My knee never really recovered from that injury, and neither did my psyche.

Sheldon Stone's wife, Esther, threw a surprise birthday party for Sheldon that year. I didn't want to attend, but she finally convinced me. I remember what I gave him: a Yankee compass that was cracked. I told him, "This reminds me of myself. Here's a broken Yankee compass from a broken Yankee ballplayer." Sheldon, Esther, and Marty Appel did everything they could to try to keep my spirits up. I almost alienated myself from them, but they wouldn't allow that to happen.

One evening the power went out in my neighborhood. It was 100 degrees outside and I could hear shots ringing out from the South Bronx. It was a scary night, and I pondered even scarier thoughts: Would *my* power ever come back on? My only hope was to follow the regimen the doctors recommended for rehabilitation. I was driven to the stadium on a daily basis for treatment. The team had somebody perform diathermy on my knee, and I was assisted with weightlifting as well. Every day was another day that I had to convince myself to keep up the rehab.

While the team was out of town, it was particularly rough. I listened to the road games on the radio. Broadcasters Frank Messer, Bill White, and Phil Rizzuto were the best; they mentioned my name on the air a lot during their games. They said, "We know Ron is back in New York, working out, and we can't wait for him to get better." And John Sterling, later a Yankee broadcaster who then had a show on WMCA radio, would always bring up my name, too. We became good friends.

What really saved me more than anything during my time on the designated list was my faith. I knew I was a chosen person, and so I believed that everything would eventually work out for the best. It did for my teammates in 1977. The Yankees won 100 games that season, narrowly edging the Orioles and Red Sox for the division crown. They defeated the Royals again to capture the A.L. pennant, and then bested the Dodgers, four games to two, in the World Series. Most major leaguers never get an opportunity to play in a World Series. I got my World Series ring but never actually played in the series due to my injury. After the Yankees won the championship, Gabe Paul told me that the team had decided to give me a full share of the winnings—about $20,000, a nice bonus for someone making close to $100,000 who didn't appear in a game all season long.

8

BYSTANDER AT THE BRONX ZOO

My injuries kept me from *playing* in 1976 and '77. But they did not keep me from *watching*. And it was a wild ride. As much as I wanted to stay away from the clubhouse due to my depression, I was drawn back in at times by the excitement generated by the team—both on and off the field. There was so much turmoil in the clubhouse and even in the dugout that it was amazing the Yankees won the American League pennant both years.

Thurman Munson was the leader on the field, which created some friction when George Steinbrenner—hoping to improve upon a club that had been swept in the '76 World Series—signed Reggie Jackson. We could see what Steinbrenner was trying to do: he was buying lots of players in an effort to recreate the winning Yankee tradition of old. When he got Catfish Hunter for the 1975 season, it was an unbelievable move; but when he nabbed Reggie, we didn't know exactly what to expect.

From playing against Reggie when he was with Oakland throughout the early part of his career and then Baltimore for one season in 1976, we knew the type of person he was. He was a different bird, and he had an aura surrounding him. Even with Steinbrenner and Billy Martin, our Yankee team had a great chemistry, and we weren't certain if Reggie would fit in. Wherever Reggie went, the writers followed, as he generated lots of publicity. When Reggie attempted to assume some of the leadership and attention from Thurman, he and Munson began to clash.

Thurman really got upset during spring training. We had to take a bus from Fort Lauderdale up to West Palm Beach, and no one on the team was that keen on the idea. But we had no choice—we had to take the bus. But Reggie had another idea. When the bus left, Reggie wasn't on it. Soon enough, we saw him driving with a friend in his own car, behind the bus. That upset a lot of the guys. The trend continued: When we had team meetings, Reggie would come late and bring his friends with him into the clubhouse. All of a sudden certain guys were living by their own rules. Before Reggie joined the team, Thurman made sure all the rules were followed and kept everybody in line. Once we got Reggie, though, it was Reggie's rules versus the Yankees' rules. We didn't go up to Reggie and complain, because he won a lot of ballgames for us. He was a dominating type of personality, but we had a lot of dominating personalities on that team. When you mix too many of those, you get friction. And we had it.

There was tension between Billy and Reggie as well. Reggie wouldn't go into the training room when Thurman was in there. Instead, he would usually hang out in the clubhouse. Billy would see him and make a comment like, "What the f-ck is he doing around here?" Billy was miffed because Reggie was getting so much publicity. A lot of people did not like Reggie simply because they were jealous of him. He was a superstar in Oakland, a superstar in New York—a superstar wherever he played. Deep inside, Billy was envious of Reggie because he got so much print in the New York papers. Whenever Reggie was in the clubhouse, all the writers swarmed around him. Billy might have but one or two giving him attention.

Reggie was the type of guy who would say whatever was on his mind, and sometimes it wouldn't come out the right way. And he was always there for the writers. In that sense, he was similar to me. Reggie and I always got along with each other, so I understood what Reggie was going through—even though he was a superstar and I wasn't. Reggie was always real good to me. He was black, I was Jewish, but we both got a lot of public-ity even with all those superstars on the team. I guess that's how we bonded. Reggie could have struck out four times in a game that was won by his teammates, but he would still get the head-lines. That caused some problems with his teammates. The Yankees put up with the tension because Reggie was blessed with talent. He had a God-given knack for performing in the postseason. He could go 0-for-30 to end the regular season, but then come to life in the glare of the limelight.

Unlike me, however, Reggie also had the habit of saying things that stirred up the clubhouse. When he said that he was the straw that stirs the drink, he took one step over the line. I don't think he did it on purpose, but I'm not certain that he didn't want to step on Thurman's feet. The "straw" comment broke in the newspapers during the 1976-77 offseason and was repeated in a magazine that came out at the start of spring training that year. It caused a giant rift between Reggie and Thurman. It was obvious that Reggie wanted to take the captain's role away from Thurman, but he should have known that nobody could do that.

I loved Thurman and he was one of my closest friends on the team. He was a guy I looked up to, the guy I wanted to serve under if we were going to war. Nobody else. A lot of people who respected Thurman saw Reggie's quote in the paper and got upset. The New York media magnified the quote by 1000 percent, and just like that, we had a huge problem on the team. Thurman confronted Reggie, and Billy had to intervene. He sat everybody down and tried to clear the air, which was an interesting ordeal since Billy Martin hardly fit the image of a peacemaker. He was a fighter himself, a brawler and a tough guy. He wasn't the type of guy who could be pushed around—by anyone. But yet here he was attempting to diffuse a fight instead of instigating one.

In the middle of June in 1977, we were playing a nationally televised Saturday afternoon game at Fenway Park in Boston. Our rivalry with the Red Sox was heated. When we played most other teams, our team would fraternize with the other team before the game. But we would never do such a thing against the Red Sox—the feelings were too intense. Whenever we played the Red Sox, our guys would come to the ballpark ready to fight. The fans in both cities must have felt the same way: we saw

more fights—some of them real whoppers—in the stands during Red Sox games than at any other time.

Reggie was in right field for this particular game against
our rivals, but his mind was somewhere else. Jim Rice hit a
bloop single in front of Reggie, who didn't charge the ball. Rice,
a slow runner, reached second base on the play. Billy called time
and sent Paul Blair into right field as a defensive replacement *in
the middle of the inning.* The resulting explosion was predictable.
Billy lit into Reggie when he made it to the dugout, and Reggie
screamed right back at Billy. Billy was questioning Reggie's
motives, screaming that he was trying to show him up. Reggie
retorted that Billy's drinking may have impaired his judgment.
That set off Billy, who would have come out swinging if not for
being restrained by Elston Howard and Yogi Berra. And the
entire confrontation was captured on national television.

Reggie's rage was near the surface anyway. He wanted to
bat fourth and play right field and resented Billy when he was
used as a designated hitter or placed lower in the batting order.
Reggie wasn't happy with most of his teammates, either. Reggie
being removed from the game because of his lackadaisical play
was just the tip of the iceberg. Cooler heads—namely Reggie's
teammates—prevailed in this incident. Mike Torrez, who had
also been taken out of the game, told Reggie in Spanish to cool
off. Reggie understood, ran down the tunnel, got dressed
before anybody else, and left to go to the hotel. Rumors were
flying in the papers the next day that Billy would be fired,
Reggie would be traded, or both. But Reggie told Steinbrenner
he didn't want to be responsible for any manager losing his
job—not even Billy Martin.

At the time of the incident, the Yankees were playing well, fighting for first place with the Red Sox. Steinbrenner didn't want anything to interfere with their success, so upon the team's return to New York, he held a private meeting with Reggie and Billy and then had a separate meeting with the whole team. He told the team that they didn't have to like the players on their team, but they had to perform with them. Billy never said anything more about the incident to Reggie. He put his name on the lineup card and let him go out and hit home runs to win games. A few of the writers had assignments to come into the clubhouse and see what they could stir up. They wanted to see another altercation. They didn't care if we won or not, but they wanted to see Reggie versus Billy because that sold papers.

That team earned its Bronx Zoo nickname. We did not have good chemistry, but we won anyway. I suppose that's a credit to the talent we had on that team, and to the coaching staff, who somehow managed to keep the fists from flying even if it was sometimes Billy's fists that were on the verge of being let loose. Billy often said that a manager's job is to keep the five guys who hate him from the five guys who were undecided. The first time we got Billy, in 1975, people said the younger players were going to like him, at least for a short period of time, and the older players were going to hate him. That was basically true. Billy did his own thing, which often meant getting drunk at the bars after games. After a long night, he would come to the ballpark—with his shades on to cover his eyes—when he wanted to, shut the door to his office, fill out his lineup card, and tell the players to go out and win. Dick Howser was really the guy who led the team, along with Elston Howard.

I didn't play much for Billy since I was hurt. He would have been a hard guy to play for because he was always looking over your shoulder. My approach to Billy was the same as with any manager: I tried to stay away from him. You never knew what Billy was going to say to you—especially if you had a bad ballgame. One time after a game in Baltimore, I went into a restaurant and spotted Billy at the bar, drinking up a storm. All of a sudden, he looked over and said, "Bloomie!" I didn't acknowledge him; I just left. I stayed away from managers. Whenever I went out to dinner and there was a manager or coach there, I would leave. That was the worst part of being a ballplayer: if you didn't do well and you ran into somebody who was drinking, you didn't want to have it rubbed into your face.

The Yankees harbored a lot of resentment during Billy's tenure. When we traveled, Thurman, Sparky Lyle, Ken Holtzman, and Graig Nettles would sit on one side of the plane, and Reggie and a couple of his friends would sit on the other. That sort of us-versus-them attitude broke us apart socially, but it did not bother us in the game of baseball. Sure, we battled among ourselves, but more importantly we battled other teams. The truth is, we had a team full of leaders—Hunter, Lyle, Munson, Ron Guidry, Chris Chambliss, Willie Randolph, Holtzman, Reggie, and Mickey Rivers—and they rose to the occasion when it mattered most.

George and Billy were always fighting, too. George was a winner and Billy was a winner. The only thing George saw was a "W" for "win." If he saw an "L," it was somebody else's fault. George called Billy many times during games and told him to put somebody in. It happened so often that many times Billy wouldn't let anyone answer the phone. He knew it was from upstairs, not from the bullpen. Steinbrenner was just a hands-on type of owner, similar to Charley Finley in Oakland or Ted Turner in Atlanta. He used to be an athlete himself, and a coach at Northwestern and Michigan. That lent George what he felt was expertise, and he believed that ownership should get involved. But Billy didn't agree, and that's why he quit or was fired so many times. George never hesitated to change managers, pitching coaches, or players in an effort to win. Many of the changes George made bothered Billy—mainly because he wasn't informed about the moves in advance. Even before Reggie Jackson was signed, it was obvious Billy was not happy about it. But he knew what was coming, since George wined and dined Reggie all over the city before convincing him to sign a month after the 1976 World Series. George also signed off on two Gabe Paul trades that irked Billy. The first one involved two of the manager's pet players, Oscar Gamble and Fred Stanley. The deal sent Gamble, LaMarr Hoyt, a minor leaguer, and $200,000 to the Chicago White Sox for Bucky Dent, which in turn knocked Stanley out of the starting shortstop's job. The other trade was a swap with the A's: Dock Ellis for Mike Torrez. Martin liked Ellis, who had won 17 games in his only full year with the Yankees. But he was an outspoken guy who wore an earring, things that did not endear him to Gabe.

The Dent trade almost backfired before it happened; Chicago insisted that Ron Guidry be included, but Gabe refused. The fact that he was still able to get his man was a tribute to Gabe's expertise as an executive. The only thing he couldn't do was please his manager. Martin was already miffed about having Holtzman on his team. Without Billy's blessing, Kenny had come to the Yankees from Baltimore during the 1976 season. Although he had pitched well for the Oakland A's when they won three straight World Series, Kenny wasn't used by the Yankees in either the 1976 or '77 World Series. I wonder whether the fact that he was Jewish had anything to do with Billy's decision to bypass him. But it did seem strange.

With Holtzman out of favor, Hunter nursing a foot injury, and Don Gullett (signed as a free agent) having problems with his shoulder, the Yankees seemed unlikely to survive a three-way divisional title chase with the Baltimore Orioles and Boston Red Sox. But Ron Guidry became the ace of the staff in his first full season, posting a 16-7 record and 2.82 ERA, and Ed Figueroa and Torrez were both dependable starters. Sparky Lyle posted 13 wins, 26 saves, and a 2.17 ERA in relief—numbers that in 1977 made him the first American League relief pitcher to win a Cy Young Award.

The offense was potent as well: Rivers and Randolph reached base often, setting the table for the heart of our order—Reggie, Thurman, and Graig. All three of our big boppers knocked in at least 100 runs that year, and Chambliss added 90. Carlos May and Jimmy Wynn handled the DH duties early in the season, with Lou Piniella and Cliff

Johnson sharing the job during the second half. We even briefly tried Dave Kingman at DH after he came aboard late in the year.

It took a while for the team to get moving in '77. In fact, it didn't really happen until the second half. That's when the Yankees took command with 40 wins in 50 games. The team wound up with 100 wins to finish just ahead of Baltimore and Boston, tied for second at two and a half games back. For the second straight year, we beat the Royals in a five-game Championship Series to take the pennant. Then we beat the Los Angeles Dodgers in a six-game World Series, making the Yankees world champions for the first time in 15 years. It was a year of stars; the Yankees had a star at nearly every position and Yankee Stadium hosted its third All-Star Game that summer.

Thurman was the brightest star in the ALCS with five RBI. But in the World Series, Reggie was a one-man show despite more impressive hitting from Munson. Reggie not only hit .450, but he also set Series records with five home runs, 10 runs scored, and 25 total bases. Reggie finished with a flourish, hitting three home runs in the last game off three different pitchers. It was a great performance; I wish I had been in uniform so I could have been in his receiving line at home plate. Thurman was being sarcastic when he dubbed Reggie "Mr. October"—claiming that Jackson only chose to hit in October—but the nickname fit. Reggie was at his best when the pressure was most intense. With 1,000 reporters, 55,000 fans in the ballpark, and millions more watching on TV, Reggie found that extra adrenaline.

Few baseball players have ever enjoyed days like that. I know I never did.

9

TEAMMATES TO REMEMBER

During the Seventies, ballplayers weren't as spoiled as they are today. When we played on the road, we had to share our hotel room with a roommate. I had some famous roommates during my stay with the Yankees, including Mickey Mantle, Thurman Munson, Bobby Bonds, and Sparky Lyle, and some infamous ones, like Mike Kekich. Sharing rooms and riding to games together allowed us to become pretty close friends off the field and helped us transcend the category of teammates.

Even though I unintentionally ruffled some feathers, I did have a lot of friends on the team. Thurman, however, was my best friend. We were roommates on the road and lived together in the Holiday Inn in Paramus, New Jersey. We were also room-mates for a year during spring training in Fort Lauderdale. We palled around together and always ate together on the road. His wife, Diane, and my wife at the time, Mara, became friends.

When they visited us on the road, Thurman stayed in one hotel room with his wife, and Mara and I shared a separate room. But we would often spend time together, and we all went to the stadium together before games.

Thurman grew up in Canton, Ohio, married his high school sweetheart, and went to Kent State. He was an excellent all-around athlete who could play football and basketball as well as baseball. And, as I've already discussed, he was a great leader, the sort of guy teammates cling to. But Thurman was a unique person, too. He wasn't as extroverted as I was, but he was friendly. Once he put that uniform on, though, he changed into a different type of person. He was a hothead, a very intense guy. I recall one occasion when he made a ground-ball out in a key situation and was so disgusted that he angrily tossed the bat toward the dugout and hit Ralph Houk in the head. Ralph was picking up pebbles like he always did, and had one of his feet on the top step of the dugout, watching the game and spitting tobacco juice. Ralph was a tough guy who never said anything, but after Thurman slung his bat and hit him in the noggin, we could see the veins sticking out of Ralph's neck. It would have knocked out anybody else, but Ralph just stood there looking really pissed off. But he wouldn't say anything. That had to be one of Thurman's most embarrassing moments, but he was just reacting like the competitor he was.

Unlike me, Thurman didn't care about the press, and so he didn't treat the writers all that well. He let me do my own thing, though. There were other people on the team who threw things at me or made me try to make a mistake while I was being interviewed. They did it in fun, but I also think they did it because of all the attention I received. Thurman never bothered me.

He helped me out on many occasions, and when I could return the favor, I did. During one off-season, I met Nat Tarnopol, the owner of Brunswick Records, an old record company that released a lot of early rock 'n roll records in the Fifties and soul and R&B in the Sixties. He not only owned that label, but he also represented Jackie Wilson, Soupy Sales, and other celebrities. Nat was Jewish, and his parents wanted him to become a rabbi. But he wasn't interested; instead he went into the music business and made a fortune. He looked up to me as a fellow Jewish role model, and we often went to dinner at the Stage Deli or hung out at his house after games. I met the Temptations, Four Tops, Jackie Wilson, Clyde Davis, and many others through Nat.

To me, Nat was like a brother. He even wanted to buy the Yankees because they weren't playing me against lefthanded pitchers. He wanted to buy the team and bring in Dick Williams as manager. He and George Steinbrenner never got along real well because they were competitors when the Yankees were up for sale. And Nat's group lost out.

On one occasion, while we were hanging out at his house, he said to me, "We gotta get you a new car. Your car is too big." I was driving a Tornado that I had bought from an Oldsmobile dealership on Jerome Avenue. It was my first car. Nat and I got into his car and headed to Peppy Motors in Mt. Vernon. I admired a silver Mercedes Benz SL with a price tag of $12,000—a lot of money back then. He said, "You like this car? Who wouldn't? It's yours—I just bought it for you."

A few days later, I drove it home and Mara went nuts. From that day on, that's the car I drove. Everybody in Riverdale knew that I had a silver SL. Thurman was shocked, too, when he saw the car and said, "I have to meet that guy." So I introduced him to Nat and they became real good friends.

I was devastated when Thurman died in a plane crash during the 1979 season. I couldn't bring myself to attend his funeral. All the Yankees players were going to be there, and I knew it would be an emotional and uncomfortable time for me. That's not to say that I haven't moved on. I enjoy seeing most of my former teammates nowadays, but I sure miss Thurman.

I was also good friends with Bobby Bonds, whose tenure with the Yankees lasted but one year, 1975—although, I have to admit, I was shocked when the Yankees acquired him. It felt like the Yankees had traded Mickey Mantle when they sent Bobby Murcer to the Giants. Murcer was a super ballplayer, one of our leaders, and a player the fans adored. But Bonds soon won me over. Before the first home game that '75 exhibition season, Bonds entered the stadium with all his things in a Giants duffel bag. There were tons of reporters there to meet him. I went right up him, shook his hand, and we hit it off right away. Later that day, we got to talking on the bench, and he kidded me about my eating—he knew about my reputation. But then he turned serious and said he didn't have a place to stay. I told him I could help him get an apartment in my building. And I told him not to worry, that I would go with him and take care of everything. Chris Chambliss was living there, too, along with a few other teammates. Willie Mays, who had recently ended his playing career with the Mets, had the penthouse in the building and the two knew each other from their days as Giants. But Bobby eventually settled on another building.

It didn't take long for Bonds to feel comfortable in New York. We spent a lot of time together off the field, roomed together on the road, and became good friends. I really cared for him. I was the first guy to call him "B.B.," a nickname all the guys used after that. He was a fantastic athlete with a wonderful attitude, but he had some personal problems. He drank a little, and I took care of him whenever he wasn't feeling good, making sure he was okay when he came to the ballpark. By the start of the game, he was reloaded and ready to go.

He did the same for me the one time I got drunk. We were down in spring training and I had too much to drink. Bobby, Thurman, and Herm Schneider helped me make it back to the hotel in Fort Lauderdale. The next day, we were supposed to fly to San Juan, Puerto Rico, for a special game in honor of Roberto Clemente. I was sick for six days with alcohol poisoning, and I was useless on the field. I think I struck out 15 times over the next three games. I had never been drunk before and have never been drunk since. Bobby took good care of me over those six days, and I thanked him for that. I was upset when he got traded to the Angels following the '75 season.

I met Bobby's son, Barry, quite a few times. He came to the clubhouse when we played in Oakland, as Barry lived in San Francisco at the time. He was just a little boy playing Little League baseball. A few years later, I remember Bobby telling me to look out for his son, because he was going to take the majors by storm. Barry was in college at the time, playing for Arizona State.

"Nobody has talent like you, Bobby," I said to him. "You run the best, you have a great arm, you have a great body, and you're strong as a bull. Nobody can top that."

Bobby disagreed. "My son is better than I am," he said. "He has more talent than I do."

"There's no way in the world," I replied.

But I was wrong: Barry was not only better than Bobby, but he was better than everyone else, too. Barry featured the same awesome combination of power and speed as his dad. Bobby was a three-time member of the 30-30 club—at 30 steals and 30 home runs in the same season. Barry bested him in that category, notching four 30-30 seasons and one 40-40 season. Like father, like son, as they say.

Scott McGregor's Yankee tenure was even shorter than Bobby's stay. A lefthanded pitcher from California, Scott and I met during spring training in the mid-Seventies and became good friends. He would come down to Atlanta before spring training, visit for a while, and then head to Fort Lauderdale with me. He never pitched for the Yankees, though. Early in the 1976 season—before he had been called up to the majors—he was traded to Baltimore with Rudy May, Tippy Martinez, Dave Pagan, and Rick Dempsey for Ken Holtzman, Doyle Alexander, Grant Jackson, and Ellie Hendricks. It turned out to be one of the few Gabe Paul deals that didn't work out best for the Yankees.

Larry Gura, who pitched for the Yankees from 1974-75, and I were also close friends. We roomed together a little bit, and like so many of my friends from that time, we loved to go out to eat together. I was upset when he left as a free agent, but he went on to have some good years with Kansas City.

Catfish Hunter was another one of my favorite teammates. We were both Southern boys with a twang in our voice. People even thought I looked like Catfish, as we both had floppy, sandy-colored hair and mustaches. We had a good relationship—even though I hit a home run against him in 1974. The night the Yankees signed him, Marty Appel and Sheldon Stone were at my house in Riverdale for a New Year's Eve party. When George Steinbrenner called to tell us the news, I went to the stadium with Marty for the press conference.

Catfish and I hit it off right away. I showed him the best restaurants and clothing stores, and we bonded quickly. He was the type of guy who took the world by its tail and did everything that came naturally to him. He went back to his hometown of Hereford, North Carolina, in the off-season, but took the time to make it to the baseball camp I used to put on. I said, "How much should I pay you?" But he wouldn't take a penny. He helped me so much at those camps, and today I honor his memory by doing a lot for ALS, also known as Lou Gehrig's Disease.

Another one of my favorite teammates was shortstop Gene Michael, who played for New York from 1968-74 and later served as manager and general manager for the team. He was an intelligent, good-fielding infielder who didn't hit very much. Everybody loved "Stick." You couldn't find a nicer human being—although he wasn't without a sense of humor. Every time I see him, he reminds me of the fact that I blew his one chance at a triple play. The batter hit a line drive to Gene at short for the first out. He then stepped on second to force out the baserunner and threw to first to nab the third out. I was playing first, and I dropped his throw. He never let me forget that.

During the off-season, he played on my basketball team. Billed as the "Boomer All-Stars," we played about 30 games against the faculties of local high schools. We gave most of the proceeds to charity, but made a little cash ourselves. In addition to Stick, our players included Chris Chambliss, Rusty Torres, Roy White, Rudy May, Walt "No-Neck" Williams, Jeff Torborg, and Elston Howard. Gene truly was a great athlete; he could have easily played professional basketball, and I was glad to have him on my team.

In 1974, Stick's last year as a player with the Yankees, Lou Piniella arrived from Kansas City. Lou was the most unbelievable guy I had ever seen. He was not only a talented hitter and a team leader, but also a brash guy who would say anything at any time. He was intense, and had a reputation for tearing up the clubhouse. He broke a lot of lights and water coolers in his time. If he struck out at the plate, he'd practice his batting stance out in left field the next inning. But he had a fun side, too, just like Sparky Lyle. Sparky and I roomed together on occasion, and he always made sure to make my birthday a memorable one.

Life at the ballpark was never dull during the time I was with the Yankees. Something was always going on. Pranks were always popular, especially with guys like Fritz Peterson, Mike Kekich, Stan Bahnsen, and Mel Stottlemyre on the team. The practical jokers didn't get me too often, but I sure remember the times when they did. There was always a watermelon in the clubhouse, and I had a reputation for eating two or three watermelons in one sitting. When I spotted a watermelon in the clubhouse one day, my eyes lit up. I sat down and dug in. Pretty soon, though, I started to feel a little odd, as if I was getting drunk. After a few more bites, I had a major buzz. I didn't know it, but Dick Tidrow had injected some grain alcohol in the watermelon. I admit it, they got me good that time—especially since I wasn't a drinker.

By comparison, however, that watermelon prank wasn't nearly as cruel as some of the others my teammates pulled on each other. One time we were at the airport, preparing to board the plane for a road trip, when Stan and Mel grabbed Kekich's bags, took them to an international claim place, and had them flown to Germany. Kekich didn't have his clothes for a week; it took that long to get his luggage back.

Kekich also had an adventure with a new waterbed he had purchased while on the road in Milwaukee. He stashed the mattress—minus the water—in his locker for safe keeping. But Fritz, Stan, and Mel swiped it and bribed the flagpole guy in Milwaukee to fly it under the American flag. We're in the middle of The National Anthem when everybody in the dugout noticed the waterbed flying under the flag. Jim Turner was our pitching coach then and he knew something was wrong. He really gave it to the culprits, but the rest of us had a good laugh.

It was a common practice while on the road to order all kinds of room-service food and have it billed to the rookies on the club. The rookies often had to pay the tab on long-distance phone calls as well. But "rookie" sometimes applied to veterans who were new to the team. Thurman Munson got together with a couple of guys and burned Reggie Jackson's clothes in the middle of the clubhouse while he was out taking batting practice. He got a little mad, but we didn't care.

Sparky Lyle was the biggest jokester on the team. If it was your birthday, Sparky would be sure to celebrate by sitting on your birthday cake. On my birthday I brought in a cake, and I received a few more from fans. I brought them all down to Pete Sheehy in the clubhouse. I was in the training room when I heard a big commotion out in the clubhouse: Sparky had sat on all the birthday cakes bare-assed.

The stunt made it into the paper and became a big joke. Whenever anybody got a cake, he sat on it. One time someone sent a cake with six or seven nails in it. We knew about the nails and made sure that Sparky didn't take a big jump into that cake. When he did sit on it, though, it was the funniest thing in the whole world. He felt the nails and jumped right up.

Catfish got in on the fun as well. He gave hotfoots to the writers when they weren't looking. Some of the guys would put bubble bath into the whirlpool so the suds would overflow and flood the whole area. And we'd lock the bathroom stalls so people couldn't get out. On airplanes, the victims might get stuck inside the bathroom for two-and-a-half hours. Guys would even put atomic balm inside your jock. If you put it on, it would stay with you for a week, burning the fool right out of you.

Gene Michael was wise to this trick, so before he got dressed, he would inspect his uniform with a stick. Gene hated bugs and creepy crawlers, so guys would often hide insects in his uniform. One day, someone found a big praying mantis at the stadium and put it in Gene's glove. When you played, your glove was always at the top of the dugout, so you just grabbed it and trotted out to your position. Gene didn't put the glove on until he got out to shortstop. He put it on, felt the praying mantis, threw the glove 15 or 20 feet into the air, and started screaming. Everybody died laughing.

Phil Rizzuto hated bugs, too. On Jake Gibbs Night at the ballpark, Rizzuto had to speak from a field microphone behind home plate. But one of his teammates got there first and scotch-taped a cricket to the mike. When Phil saw it, he went nuts, threw the microphone down, and ran all the way to second base.

Even the clubhouse guys got into the act. We'd get messages at our lockers that read "Call G. Raff or D. Lion." The unsuspecting player would dial the number—usually the number of the *real* Bronx Zoo—and ask to speak with G. Raff or D. Lion, even after they realized they were calling the zoo. We were a bunch of wild and crazy guys. It kept everybody loose. But when the practical jokers were out in the field, they did their job. Inside the clubhouse was a different story—we didn't have any idea what was happening.

That was never more obvious than during the 1973 season: Steinbrenner purchased the Yankees, I became the first designated hitter, and Mike Kekich traded his family for Fritz Peterson's. No joke! Kekich and Peterson lived in the same town, were best friends, and their families were very close—which made the ordeal all the more bizarre. I had an inkling something was going on the year before, when Kekich was my roommate. About four o'clock in the morning, Mike and I were asleep when the phone rang. I was half-asleep, but I do remember that phone call: Marilyn Peterson had called Mike. When he finished the conversation, he said, "Goodbye. I love you."

I love you? The words stuck with me. I thought maybe I was dreaming, but it sure sounded real. The next spring, when I showed up in Fort Lauderdale, Mel Stottlemyre and Thurman Munson came up to me and said, "Have you heard?" I said, "Heard what?" They told me that Kekich and Peterson had swapped wives, and that it was going to be a huge deal in the press. Sure enough, ABC, NBC, and *60 Minutes* were all present at our spring training. The upshot was that Kekich and Peterson not only traded families—*including kids*—but traded their bank accounts, too. Even the family dogs were not spared. And the longtime best friends weren't speaking to each other anymore.

We were all in shock, but I could picture Kekich doing something like that. In put the Yankees in an awkward spot. They knew that they couldn't keep both guys, so they traded Kekich to Cleveland, parting with a 28-year-old lefthanded pitcher of promise. When Mike got traded, we began to see Fritz in Yankee Stadium with Susan Kekich, Mike's former wife. But we never saw the kids with them.

Eventually, Kekich and Marilyn Peterson's relationship failed, but Fritz and Susan Kekich made a go of it. A year after the story broke, Peterson also was traded to Cleveland. But Kekich had already jumped to the Japanese major leagues by that time. What a crazy story that was, but hanging around the Yankees in the Seventies, one came to expect such wild times.

10

COUNTRY COUSINS

I did something unusual for a power hitter over the course of my career: I walked more often than I struck out. Check the numbers: 140 walks and 134 strikeouts in eight seasons. I ended my career with a solid on-base percentage of .360 thanks to all of those walks. I had a decent slugging percentage of .473 as well. In the batter's box, things came naturally to me. I was a great fastball hitter, and most pitchers were fastball pitchers when I played. I hit many of my home runs off fastballs.

Every hitter has a favorite pitcher, a guy he views as his "country cousin" because he looks forward to seeing him. I hit only 52 home runs in my career, but six of them came against guys who wound up in the Hall of Fame: Jim Palmer, Nolan Ryan, Fergie Jenkins, Catfish Hunter, and Gaylord Perry. Three more came against non-Hall of Famers who won Cy Young Awards during their careers: Denny McLain, Jim Perry, and Steve Stone.

I hit my first home run against Pete Broberg of the Washington Senators in 1971, when I was 23 years old. He was a big guy from Florida and a No. 1 draft pick like I was. In the paper the next day, one writer celebrated my first homer with the line, "The Southern Jew hit his first home run." I hit another home run against Broberg the following year.

The White Sox were involved in my first home run as a DH. They played victim to my bat when I took Steve Stone deep on July 11, 1973. Hitting against Steve had an added dimension for me since we were both Jewish. Five seasons after I took him deep, we would be teammates in Chicago.

Gaylord Perry was always accused of throwing a spitball or Vaseline ball—he even admitted it after his career was over—but I hit him pretty well, especially when his pitches stayed up a little bit. When he kept the ball down, he was tough to hit. I was a full-time designated hitter when I hit two home runs in a game against Gaylord when he was pitching for Cleveland at the end of the 1974 season. It was the first year the Indians played in Jacobs Field, a much better ballpark to hit in than Municipal Stadium. Gaylord was a tough old guy at the age of 36; the next time I faced him, he gave me some chin music. I remember the two-homer game well because I also hit a home run off Tom Buskey as a pinch-hitter in the second game of the September doubleheader that day.

Everyone knew that Gaylord was doctoring the ball, but we never said anything about it. During an Old Timers game long after he had retired, Gaylord told us how he did it: he put Vaseline under the brim of his cap. As he would sweat, he would wipe his brow and remove his hat. In the process, he would get some of the cream on his fingers. The resulting pitch was just incredible; it sometimes dropped two feet. He said it was a sinker, but no one ever threw a natural sinker like *that*.

The Perry family was pretty good to me: I hit a home run against Gaylord's brother Jim when he was pitching for Minnesota. Good pitchers like the Perrys often give up lots of home runs because they are always around home plate. Their secret to success is giving up those home runs with no one on base.

Bert Blyleven once gave up 50 home runs in a season—a major-league record—but he drove me nuts. The first game I faced him during my rookie season, I struck out three times. He was just a 20-year-old at the time. The next time I faced him— less than two weeks later—I got three singles against him. But I never hit a home run against him. He had the best curveball, by far, that I've ever seen in baseball.

One guy I owned was Dick Tidrow, who later became my teammate with the Yankees. My contract could have been a whole lot richer if I *only* hit against Tidrow. When he was with the Indians early in his career, he was used primarily as a starter. He threw a pretty good sinker, but he would often try to throw me inside. He couldn't throw the ball too far inside because my bat was just a little too quick. The result was three home runs for me—all coming in the month of September in 1973. I hit more home runs against Tidrow than against any other pitcher.

Unlike almost everybody else, I loved to hit against Nolan Ryan. I was comfortable in the batter's box against him because I had quick hands and I knew I could catch up to his heat. I hit a solo home run against him in the first inning of a midsummer game at Yankee Stadium in 1972, and my teammates proceeded to do their part in knocking Ryan out of the game in the fourth inning. My shot went three-quarters of the way into the upper deck. I think that's when Phil Rizzuto and Bill White started calling me "The Boomer." I had a big swing, so most of my home runs were booming shots.

Another of my country cousins was Jim Palmer, who won three Cy Young Awards during his career, and nearly won three others. Palmer's delivery came right over the top, and he threw extremely hard. I did especially well against him in Memorial Stadium in Baltimore, but my home run against him came at Yankee Stadium in 1972, a month before my home run against Ryan.

There was a little extra incentive for me when I faced Ryan or Palmer, just as there was when we played the Red Sox. Those guys were the best pitchers of their generation, and so that gave me the additional drive I needed to really excel against them. The same goes for Catfish Hunter. While Catfish was still with Oakland, I connected against him, too. Catfish was the type of pitcher with a serious competitive streak—he would not give in to any hitter. But he played to my strength, which was the fastball. Three days before I connected against Catfish in 1974, I teed off against Fergie Jenkins at Shea Stadium. He was another hard thrower, but as they say, the harder they throw, the farther they go.

One of my more memorable home runs came in 1973 against another old teammate, Mike Kekich, after the Yankees dealt him to Cleveland. Ralph Houk let me step in against Kekich, a lefthander, and I hit a bomb off him. The writers came in after the ballgame and said to Houk, "Can't you give Blomberg a chance to hit against lefthanded pitchers?" Houk's answer was evasive, and only added to my frustration as a platoon hitter. Since I rarely hit against lefties, my only home runs against lefthanders came against Kekich and Bill Butler. But I actually hit a couple of lefties pretty well. I got some hits against Vida Blue, Mickey Lolich, and Paul Splittorff.

I hit a few dramatic home runs late in games, and I also hit quite a few three-run homers. But the only grand slam I hit in my career also happened to be the last home run I hit: against Alan Wirth of the A's in a game in Oakland on September 19, 1978. That came during my final season in the majors, when I was with the White Sox. With one out in the eighth inning and the Sox down 4-2, I cranked a Wirth pitch out of the park for the game-winning hit. Less than two weeks later, my big-league career would be finished. But what a way to go out!

MOVING ON

When I became eligible for free agency after the 1977 season, I told Sheldon Stone that I wanted to leave New York. It would be the toughest thing in the world for me, but it was necessary for my mental state. I wanted a fresh start. There were a couple of people on the Yankees who made me feel a little guilty about my decision to leave, and there were some comments from players in the papers. They said I had disappointed the team, the players, and the fans. But I didn't see it that way. I had played hard every time I stepped on the field; I just suffered from some poor luck with my injuries.

My wife at the time, Mara, and I also had a new son, Adam, a beautiful little boy. Having him in my life really helped me through my final two rough seasons as a Yankee. He was also a big reason that I wanted a change in scenery. I needed to improve my mental health so that I could be a good dad.

When I announced that I was leaving New York, I received a wonderful outpouring of support from fans who pleaded with me not to go. People would stand outside my building in Riverdale with signs that read, "DON'T GO, BLOMBERG." But to counter that, articles appeared in the *New York Post* and *Daily News* with harsh quotes from George Steinbrenner and Gabe Paul. The Yankees were not pleased with my decision to leave. In fact, George and Gabe were livid. They contacted me and said, "How in the world can you do this? We stayed behind you, we paid for your operations, we gave you all the leeway you wanted, and we wanted you to be a part of the team. We kept you on the roster—we did everything for you. We need you."

Gabe wanted to know the details of the contract I was offered by the Chicago White Sox. When I told him, he changed his tune, saying, "You did the right thing. I can't blame you for signing there. We would've offered a one-year contract for $55,000 and it wouldn't have been guaranteed."

I started to have second thoughts about leaving the only team I had known, but then I said to myself, "I've got to do this. I've got to have a clean slate." When I opted for free agency, I was concerned that I wouldn't generate any interest from other teams. After all, I had barely played in two seasons. So I was surprised when eight or nine teams drafted negotiating rights to sign me. Five or six of those teams were serious—each of them willing to take a gamble on me. The Mets wanted me very badly, so I had a chance to stay in New York, and the Braves wanted me because I was from Atlanta. The Braves eventually dropped out but the Mets and White Sox went down to the wire. But I knew that if I went to the Mets, I really wasn't solving my problem; I would still be in New York. I would see my teammates during the off-season.

Still, I entertained the Mets' offer. We met on Wall Street with M. Donald Grant, the team's chairman of the board. He came across as a businessman, and I didn't care for the formality. But the offer wasn't bad: a one-year, $100,000 contract without a full no-trade clause. After mulling it over for a while, I decided not to accept it. Jumping to the Yankees' crosstown rivals just wasn't right.

The White Sox offer was much better: it was a four-year, guaranteed contract with a $100,000 bonus just for signing. The total value was $750,000. The annual average of $162,500 was three times higher than my best annual salary with the Yankees ($57,000 in 1973). In addition to the money, I went with the White Sox because of Bill Veeck, their fabulous owner, and Roland Hemond, his general manager and one of the true gentlemen of the game. When I met with Veeck, he made me feel like part of a family again. "Look at my leg," he said to me, referring to his wooden leg. "Everybody gave up on me because of my leg. Look where I am now. I'm the talk of baseball."

I could see why Veeck was called "Sportshirt Bill." He was a regular guy. The only thing fake about him was his leg, which he lost during World War II. He had an ashtray built into the leg. I know that because I saw him use it to put out a cigarette during our negotiations. I figured if he could walk with a wooden leg, I could walk with two bad legs.

Veeck truly wanted me on his team, and that showed through the course of our negotiations. Veeck told me that he remembered scouting me when I was playing high school ball in

Atlanta. "You are a great athlete," he said. "We had you pegged as our No. 1 choice." He not only made the best contract offer, but he also agreed that I would not have to submit to a physical. They read doctors' reports on my knee and shoulder and felt secure that I would be good as new. Veeck also mentioned that he had signed a third baseman named Eric Soderholm who had a bad knee but worked hard to overcome the ailment and ended up having a good season with the White Sox.

Just as it was in New York, my religion appealed to Veeck as well. He told me there were other Jews on the team, including Steve Stone and Ross Baumgarten. "With your personality," Veeck told me, "and all the Jewish people in Chicago, you're going to be a perfect fit."

Veeck was a good salesman, of course. He wanted me to help replace the power he lost when Richie Zisk and Oscar Gamble left as free agents after the 1977 season. Both of them had hit 30-plus homers for the Sox that year. They were "rent-a-players" for Veeck; he acquired them just before they could become free agents and command salaries he couldn't afford. There was no way I could have replaced both guys, but Veeck hoped I wouldn't have to. He had also picked up my old Yankee roommate, Bobby Bonds, from the Angels during the winter.

Upon signing with Chicago, the team sent me to a rehab center during the winter and I came back strong as a bull. In spring training, I was hitting the ball well. I made several appearances on a radio show hosted by Bill Veeck and his wife, Mary Frances. I enjoyed all the clowning around; it was therapeutic for me after two years on the shelf.

I found Chicago to be a beautiful city with terrific people, including a large Jewish population. All the synagogues contacted me and I visited many of them. I met a lot of people in Skokie, the home of many Holocaust survivors, and found a condo in a very exclusive address right downtown, not far from the Chicago River. My next-door neighbor was Natalie Cole, and my son, Adam, played with her daughter. Off the field, I became friendly with Lee Stern, who owned the Chicago Sting soccer team. Mara and I used to visit his house in the suburbs. He owned a place on the Chicago Board of Trade and I was planning to get involved with that. But I changed my mind after he was shot by the Mafia. I decided it was probably best to concentrate on baseball.

White Sox manager Bob Lemon had been the pitching coach of the Yankees in 1976, so I was already familiar with him. He brought me into his office and said, "I remember watching you in New York. Don't worry about anything. You are going to play here and you won't have any pressure." I was friendly with many of my new teammates, including a lot of the black and Hispanic guys on the team: Ralph Garr, Chet Lemon, Lamar Johnson, and Jorge Orta. I was closest to Bobby Molinaro; he and I would have fun arguing over whether to go out to eat at a Kosher deli or a pizza joint.

But to my dismay, I didn't blend in to the Chicago clubhouse as well as I had hoped. There were four or five guys on the team who never spoke to me and would not associate with me outside of the ballpark. Even though he was Jewish, my relationship was not good with pitcher Steve Stone. He did his own thing. In addition, there were a lot of born-again Christians on the team who held regular prayer meetings. They didn't accept that I was Jewish and didn't want me to get involved, even though the meetings were supposed to be nondenominational.

The atmosphere in Chicago was the opposite of what it was in New York. When I left New York, players were driving Rolls Royces or Mercedes; but in Chicago, everybody had a station wagon. Judging by my hot hitting in spring training and my great Opening Day game, my results on the field looked to be the opposite, too, of what I had experienced over my last three years in New York. Now wearing No. 10 instead of the No. 12 I had worn with the Yankees, I fared well on the first day of the '78 season against my old archrivals, the Red Sox. I hit fifth in the order as the designated hitter, right behind Bonds. I came up to bat in the bottom of the ninth inning against reliever Dick Drago and tied the game with a solo home run into the upper deck of Comiskey Park. It was a packed house that day—over 50,000 in attendance—and the crowd went nuts. Chet Lemon followed me with a single, and Wayne Nordhagen doubled him home to give us the win, 6-5.

The response in the papers was enthusiastic: headlines read, "Blomberg is Our Messiah" and "Blomberg Signing is Right Move for Bill Veeck." But the euphoria was short-lived. I knew that my shoulder still wasn't right, as I couldn't throw the ball real hard. I started receiving injections for the shoulder in spring training because it was inflamed. My knees weren't good either, although I was running pretty well. But I had to ice them down before every game. Simply put, I knew I was breaking down.

My problems in Chicago began with the trainer. He alienated me from everybody on the team from the minute I arrived. On the first day of spring training, I needed some tape for my blisters, but he wouldn't look at me or talk to me. If I was first in line to get taped or to go in the whirlpool, he would take me fourth or fifth. He was a problem, and anytime I needed attention for a health-related issue, he made me feel like a second-class citizen. If I needed ice for my knee or shoulder, he made me wait. Then he would give me a towel full of ice and then start questioning me right away: "What's your problem?" He was polite to everybody else, but he treated me like a schmuck. I don't know what he had against me, but he acted like I wasn't even there.

Physically, I wasn't. I was probably 70 percent healthy. With the type of injuries I had, they couldn't scope my knee or my shoulder; the only option was to cut into them. The usual recovery period, in both cases, was about a year. I was getting cortisone shots every four or five days in my shoulder, and taking an anti-inflammatory they used to give to racehorses. My knee was no better. In 1978, nobody knew what an ACL (anterior cruciate ligament) injury was or how to take care of it. It simply wasn't as easy then to come back from a knee operation. But I was trying.

I got to the ballpark at 11 o'clock in the morning for a seven o'clock game and iced my shoulder for three hours. I repeated the treatment after the game. Despite the ailments, I got off to a relatively good start. I hit three homers in April, including two in my first three games. But I hit just two more home runs the rest of the season. My average at the end of the year was only .231, by far the worst of my career. My playing time decreased significantly in the second half of the season.

The White Sox had won 90 games in 1977, but were struggling in '78. Lemon, who was in his second season after replacing Paul Richards, was one of Veeck's old cronies. He was an easygoing, laid-back type of manager who just couldn't light a fire under the White Sox. At midseason, he was replaced by Larry Doby. Lemon then succeeded Billy Martin as Yankee manager three weeks later and went on to lead the Yankees to a 48-20 record down the stretch and a World Series title. Doby had been the majors' second black player, after Jackie Robinson, and was now the second black manager, after Frank Robinson. To me, he was just another manager—and merely average. He didn't do much for the team, and lasted only the rest of that season. The Sox wound up fifth in the seven-team American League West with 71 victories.

The next spring, Don Kessinger, a light-hitting 36-year-old shortstop, became our player-manager. It didn't help my situation at all. He had been great to me when he was the shortstop, but things changed when he became the manager. I never figured out what happened to change his tune. It was obvious in spring training that I could still run well, but I couldn't swing a bat with power, and I was used to doing that my whole career. Bill Veeck asked how the shoulder was and I told him the truth: it hurt. He was very apologetic: he said the Sox were trying to win and needed to release me. I'm sure Kessinger was behind that decision. I wasn't surprised when he was replaced as manager by Tony La Russa in early August.

My release came the day before the team broke camp—too late in the spring for any other team to sign me to their big-league roster. I was leading the White Sox in batting average and hitting the ball well. The Pittsburgh Pirates contacted me along with three or four other teams. But they wanted me to start in the minor leagues and work my way up from Triple-A. They already had their rosters settled. I thought the Mets might still have interest in me, but they were bitter from the year before when I didn't take their offer. Even though I thought they had a need for me, they declined to make an offer. Joe McDonald, their general manager, told me, "Sometimes the best deals are the ones you don't make."

I suddenly realized that I was finished at age 30. It was a sad discovery, as I was not leaving on my own accord. I really felt like I did not fulfill my potential, and in the process I let a lot of people down—including myself. It took me a while to get over that feeling. It was difficult to say goodbye to baseball, since I had been playing the game constantly since age eight. But keeping things in perspective, I did take with me some lovely parting gifts. My .293 career batting average was one example. My '78 season had cost me a .300 lifetime average. I had gone into that season with a .301 average, but my struggles that year caused my career average to drop eight points. But I was glad I gave the game one last shot that season. In addition to my career average, I also enjoyed a wonderful amount of positive press during my career. And, of course, I'm in the Hall of Fame as the first designated hitter.

After I retired as a player, I thought about staying in baseball. I had an opportunity to do some work for the Yankees, but I turned it down because I didn't want to travel again. I needed to stay home and be with my family. So I headed back to Atlanta to take care of my parents, who were getting along in years. To support my family, I worked with Fran Tarkenton in the insurance business and then took a job with Robert Jameson Associates, a firm that found jobs for people who wanted to switch careers—which sounded like a perfect job for someone forced to suddenly change careers.

In 1985, I started my own career consulting business, USA Career Marketing, and operated it for 10 years. It became the largest corporate outplacement firm in the southeastern United States. We trained people for jobs but did not guarantee job placement. We were not recruiters and did not tell people where to find work. One particular client whom we trained took a job that did not work out. He knew who I was so he contacted the local paper and they turned his complaint into some negative press for the company. It was the only complaint we ever received, but it was his word against my word. We had letters he sent us that he was happy with the company, but the newspaper writers chose not to review them.

I had a contract with that client but refunded his money anyway. But that one experience caused a domino effect because the paper reported that I had refunded the man's money. It said anyone who wasn't happy could ask for his or her money back.

So people with whom I *was* successful asked for their money back, as a smart business person would be inclined to do in such a circumstance. One client became ten, then fifty, then one hundred. Those people had jobs—they were executives—and I had positive letters from them all. But all of a sudden, I had to refund hundreds of thousands of dollars, and that wrecked my business. The Office of Consumer Affairs was trying to work it out so I only had to pay back a portion of the money to people who said they were not happy—even though I had documentation stating that they were content. It became a no-win situation, and I had to close the business down.

I decided to return to what I loved. I found a way to get back into baseball as a hitting instructor. I now teach kids how to hit. I coach four or five kids at an indoor batting cage in Roswell, a suburb of Atlanta. I rent the cages and work with the kids several days a week. The kids are serious about baseball, and a couple of my students have gone on to receive athletic scholarships to college.

I work with the kids as a team. That works well because they're in competition with each other instead of in individual workouts. That competition forces them to focus. It doesn't matter whether a kid is righthanded or lefthanded; either way, hitting a baseball is a very simple philosophy. You see the ball, you swing, and you hit the ball. The philosophy is simple, but the execution is not. Hitting a baseball is probably the toughest thing to do in all of sports, but I try to make it very simple for the kids. There are a few techniques that can help separate the good hitters from the poor ones—and that's what I teach.

I began teaching kids before I retired as a player. I had my own baseball camp, run by my friend Sheldon Stone at Bergen Catholic High School in Paramus, New Jersey. We had 200 to 300 kids at the camp, which was the largest day camp in the New York-New Jersey metropolitan area. Catfish Hunter made appearances there, along with Mike Vail, Ed Kranepool, and Jimmy Wynn. Years later, I got a big thrill when I found out my stockbroker had been one of my campers; he showed me his old T-shirt that read, "Ron Blomberg Baseball Camp."

In addition to my hitting clinics, I make appearances at baseball card shows, attend the Yankee Fantasy Camp, and speak at schools, synagogues, and men's clubs. Two years ago, I went to Cooperstown to participate in the special event that Marty Appel helped put together to honor Jewish ballplayers. My old Yankee teammates Ken Holtzman and Elliott Maddox were there, along with Mike Epstein, Norm Sherry, Richie Scheinblum, Norm Sherry, and Bob Tufts. About a year later, I joined Len Berman of WNBC-TV in a special program about drug abuse in baseball put together by the Weizmann Institute of Science in New York.

I stay in shape, too, although I never throw batting practice, as my shoulder is so bad that I can barely throw at all. I use pitching machines with the kids. When I see former players at Old Timers Day who are sick or overweight, I use that as motivation to stay fit. I enjoy life too much to be in poor health. I want to be more than a face on a piece of cardboard. So I work out at 6:30 every morning. I had my time in athletics and I learned how to stay healthy, if not free from injury. Even when I had serious operations on my knee and shoulder, I made a great effort to come back from those. I didn't come back as strong as I had been before, but I wasn't lacking the faith or the drive to give it a mighty try. A lot of other guys wouldn't have done that.

Today, I owe it to my family to keep in good shape. I look at my son and daughter, and they give me all the inspiration I need to keep battling the aging process.

12

THE LOVES OF MY LIFE

was given two gifts in my life: athletic ability and a small but loving family. My parents, Sol and Goldie Rae, were very supportive. They couldn't make it up to Yankee Stadium an awful lot to see me play, so they taped my games and listened to them. They gave the tapes to my friends and to my Little League managers. During the off-season, however, they did get to see me in action: I played ball in their driveway. We used a broomstick and a tinfoil ball or a wiffle ball. We drew a strike zone on the side of the carport and played Home Run Derby. I can't tell you how many times I clobbered that wiffle ball right through Marty Appel's stomach.

My parents gave up their jewelry store about 20 years ago. My mom, who was a smoker, passed away eight years later from lung cancer. Doctors operated on her and said she was doing great after the operation. But four days later, while she was in the intensive care unit, she passed away. Five years after that, my father had a stroke. He was in assisted living for a while and then had to move to a nursing home, but he's still alive.

My only sibling, a brother named Alan, was four years older than me but suffered from health problems. He was born with a heart defect, and the doctors told my parents that he would not survive his teenage years. They were right: he died at age 17 in the spring of 1961, less than six months before my Bar Mitzvah. Alan had to go to the hospital once or twice a month. One day, after I got home from a Little League game, my parents came home and said that Alan passed away. It's another example of how medicine had not caught up to current times; in today's medical world, Alan's problem could have been fixed. He was a studious guy, a very intelligent person, and we were very close. It made perfect sense to name my son, Adam, after my brother.

I started my own family while I was still in the minor leagues. I was playing for Manchester of the Eastern League, a Double-A affiliate of the Yankees, in 1969. We were in Elmira, New York, to play the Baltimore Orioles' farm team. After the game, I went to a bar called The Office with a couple of teammates. I didn't drink, but I enjoyed the company. I was talking to a few people when I spotted a woman I wanted to meet. I went up to her and said, "Are you Jewish?" She looked at me with her big eyes and said, "What do you care?" I replied, "Because I'm Jewish, too." Maybe it wasn't the best of pick-up lines, but it worked.

Due to my blond hair, blue eyes, and Southern accent, the woman didn't believe me, so she asked me to say the blessing over the wine in Hebrew. I thought it was an interesting request given the fact that we were in a bar in Elmira, but I did it without pause. She was a college student at Syracuse University—probably the most intellectual woman I have ever met—and we started dating and became good friends. Soon enough I met her parents—she comes from a great family—and she came down to Atlanta to meet my family as well. Less than a year later, I married Mara Goldsmith in October of 1970, right after her graduation from college.

Our wedding was in Elmira, but our "honeymoon" was in the Florida Instructional League, where I was due to report for the Yankees. The team only gave me four days for the wedding, so after we were married, we had to head for Clearwater, Florida, where the Yankees trained. It was a realistic transition for the wife of a soon-to-be Major League Baseball player. The baseball life is never easy for a family: half the season I was on the road. It was very, very difficult for both of us. We eventually separated when I was having problems with my shoulder toward the end of my time with the Yankees. I was going through a hard time in my life, and I didn't feel like going out or talking to anybody—not even Mara. I was struggling to learn how to just be myself again, both at the ballpark and at home. She was very supportive, as is her nature as a wonderful person, and she helped see me through it. We never yelled at each other, but we did grow apart.

When I shattered my knee, I further shattered my self-confidence. I realized I wasn't going to play till age 40; I was on the downside of my career. I accepted at that time that I had to make some changes in my life. I had to get away from my baseball life. I suggested that Mara and I go into counseling so we could divorce properly, without any screaming or acrimony. We were always friendly and the divorce did not change that. But we both needed to move on. We both lived in Atlanta, which made it easier to raise Adam. He was always No. 1 priority for both of us. We had built a new home in Atlanta, but I never lived there. I stayed with my parents while Mara, Adam, and our two dogs—Dudley and Boomer—lived in the house. We finally separated in the spring of 1979.

Despite the divorce, Mara and I raised Adam to be a terrific son. He was born in 1976, so for most of his life his parents have been divorced. But we made sure to show him when we separated that we both still loved him very much. As he grew up, Adam became a great athlete. He played basketball and ran track in high school. But whenever he played, fans always compared him to me. If he didn't do well, some people would say, "Your father did this," or "Your father did that." He didn't like that, and I don't blame him. When he went to the University of Miami, he managed the football and basketball programs and made a lot of friends. Those friends included the team doctors of the Miami Dolphins, which worked out well for him since he always wanted to be a doctor. He eventually became an anesthesiologist. Today he is one of the most caring people I have ever met, and one incredibly smart person. Adam and his fiancé are Jewish and live in a Jewish home.

Adam's mother and I are dear friends now. We would do anything for each other, and we're both happy how our lives turned out. How could we not be? After all, we raised a son whom we are very proud of.

After my divorce and retirement from baseball, I came to a crossroads in my life. I began working in the insurance business, and soon enough I met a woman who was working for a stockbroker. We met in her office, and I think it was love at first sight. Beth and I talked and began spending time together as friends. She was from Elizabethton, Tennessee—just five minutes from Johnson City, where I started my professional career. She knew everybody I knew in Johnson City. Our similarities didn't end there: both of our fathers were jewelers. But she wasn't a big baseball fan; matter of fact, she had never seen me play. But she was a college football fan, so we got along extremely well.

Beth and I have been married for 23 years now. We have a daughter named Chesley, who *is* a baseball fan and cheers loudly for the Yankees and Derek Jeter. She's now a sophomore at the University of Alabama. She's a great daughter, and a wonderful person.

I share my love of sports with both of my kids: Chesley loves Alabama football and Adam graduated from the University of Miami. So I became fans of both schools. Both of my children have accompanied me to Old Timers games in New York, and enjoy seeing their dad with his former teammates. When I go up for those games, I make a point of going to the same restaurants I enjoyed as a player. When I call for reservations, I say, "Ron Blomberg, New York Yankees." They remember me still, as I do them. Spending time in the city is probably more enjoyable than the games, since I can't see that well anymore and I'm not in great shape to play ball. But I did manage to hit a home run against Mike Torrez four or five years ago—and my son got the ball. He was the happiest guy in the world, as that was the only time he has ever seen me in action. Torrez was only throwing about 75 miles per hour, but I hadn't taken batting practice in a couple of years. He threw me a fastball and I hit it into the upper deck. The crowd loved that.

I've been living in Atlanta my entire life, but that is going to change soon. The city has gotten too big for me. I bought some land near Asheville, North Carolina, and plan to move my whole family there. My father is from that area, and I love the beautiful mountains. It's time to move to where my family's roots are, way down yonder.

13

THE GAME TODAY

The game today is so different than it was three decades ago when I played. Look no further than the subject of home runs. In the American League in the Seventies, the league leader in home runs almost always hit about 33 or so homers a season. Not until Boston's Jim Rice hit 39 in 1977 did anyone seriously threaten the 40-home run barrier. Rice knocked out 46 the following year. Compare that to today, when a player has to hit at least 45 to 50 home runs to lead the league.

It's not just a few players who are cranking out more home runs—it's everyone. In the Seventies, a team could lead the A.L. with 130 to 150 home runs, and several teams may not even break the 100 threshold. But over the past five seasons in the A.L., the league-leading team has had at least 230 homers, with several other teams breathing down its neck. The highest team total during my playing career was 213, and that was in the offensive season of '77 when the Red Sox featured a murderer's row of Rice, Carlton Fisk, Butch Hobson, Carl Yastrzemski, Fred Lynn, and George Scott.

There are several factors at play, but steroids are definitely among the bigger reasons for the offensive explosion. Today's players are not better athletes than their predecessors. Coming out of high school, I had an astounding vertical leap, I ran extremely well, I had a super arm, and I was a great hitter. I didn't hit home runs to the opposite field on a consistent basis, but I had as much power as anyone else.

As a player, I worked out all the time, but I've never gained 30 or 40 pounds of muscle. I didn't have a personal trainer when I played, but I was physically fit. It looks like some of these guys today ate their weights and digested them. They're so cut, it's amazing. If a player needs to gain 15 pounds, he can do it in a hurry. It's similar to the Atkins Diet. If a person follows Atkins for 30 days, he or she can lose 15 pounds. If a baseball player needs to gain 15 pounds of muscle in a hurry, he can do that by taking the juice. The problem is that players today have so much on the line monetarily that they think they have to perform at all costs. They adopt the attitude that "nothing is going to happen to me."

I didn't risk anything when I was a player. I wasn't playing for a four-or five-year contract, I was playing for next year's contract. And I went out on the field and did my best to compete day in and day out. When I played, I did not smoke or drink. And I did not see people on my team doing drugs. I *heard* that a few guys were doing drugs, but I never saw anything. In my day, a lot of players took greenies, a weight-loss medication that had a stimulant effect similar to a high dosage of caffeine. There's an energy drink now that has the same stuff in it as greenies.

Thirty years later, steroids have far surpassed the effects of greenies. I remember Bobby Bonds bringing his son Barry into the clubhouse to introduce him to me. Barry was six foot one and 165 pounds at the time. When he was chosen as the No. 1 draft pick of the Pirates, he was still about the same weight. He hit some home runs in his early years, but nothing close to the frequency he established late in his career. He's the same height but now he weighs around 225 pounds and looks like a weightlifter. He's gained 50 pounds of muscle weight.

I wonder how many home runs Dave Kingman could have hit if he had been on the juice. He could crush balls out of every stadium in the whole world. What about Harmon Killebrew? No one could hit a ball farther than he could. Or Willie McCovey, Mickey Mantle, Willie Stargell, and Willie Mays? Those guys would have hit 80 home runs a year. Rod Carew won a batting title in 1972 without hitting a single home run. On the juice, he might have hit .400 and averaged 20 homers a year.

I see players today hit 475-foot home runs—and they *missed* hitting the ball on the sweet spot. Guys hit 450-foot home runs to the opposite field like it's nothing. They break their bat on a swing and the ball still goes out. I feel baseball has to do something. All those records people achieved without unnatural help should mean more. The juice is allowing a lot of average players to become superstars. I don't believe that hitters today are really that much better than we were 30 years ago.

But steroids aren't the only reason for concern. The pitching talent has been diluted because of expansion, the ballparks are smaller, the balls are likely wound tighter, and the players are using maple bats. Those are not necessarily easy things to change. Major League Baseball is not going to kick four or more teams to the curb to improve the pitching talent—the players union would never agree to it. Ballparks are not going to be built with smaller dimensions in mind, because home runs bring people to the park. The answer is to take the juice away and allow baseball to come back to reality. Players won't hit the ball as far, and the home run totals will come down.

I'm glad that Major League Baseball has finally decided to take a stand against steroid offenders. It sends the right message to kids. In giving batting lessons to high schoolers, I hear them discussing how easy it is to find steroids and muscle enhancers—at health clubs or vitamin stores. They need to understand that steroids are a controlled substance. If the body is on something for a long time, it will suffer a shock reaction if it's taken away. Bodies may break down if they're not filled with steroids anymore. Look at what happened to Ken Caminiti, who admitted to using steroids and died at a very young age.

In addition to the physical harm steroids cause, what about the harm to the integrity of the game? Frank Robinson suggested that baseball should wipe out Rafael Palmeiro's records because he failed a drug test and apparently lied to Congress. But what about the others who are allegedly involved? Should Barry Bonds lose the single-season home run record and be denied the chance to challenge Hank Aaron's career record? And what about Sammy Sosa, the only man to hit 60 home runs in three different seasons? Or Mark McGwire, who got out of baseball at the right time?

But baseball's problems don't stop with steroids. There are other significant concerns as well. For one thing, an owner shouldn't be commissioner. Bud Selig, who owned the Milwaukee team, is very partial to the owners. I think they need somebody in charge who really knows the game, wants to keep it clean, and is not partial to the owners *or* the players.

Financials are another concern. Big money has been a base-ball issue for a long time. When I first came up in 1969, the owners claimed they were losing money. When they split into three divisions per league and added an extra round of playoffs in 1994, Major League Baseball claimed it was due to the own-ers' pocketbooks. But if the owners want to stop losing money, then stop handing out ridiculous contracts to players. The salaries have risen so fast that only four or five teams can go for the top free agents now. The lower-tier teams are forced to trade their best players to the highest bidder. That's the only way they will make money. And that leaves the teams with the most money to buy or trade for the best players. It's amazing that baseball has any parity between the haves and the have-nots. It's a tribute to good scouting, player development, and coaching.

Everybody playing baseball today has a chance to make good money. But the players don't know their history and that's too bad. They should look at what the Players Association has done for them over the years. In fact, they should kiss the ground that Curt Flood and Andy Messersmith walked on. Player paychecks should have a picture of Marvin Miller on them. He's the guy who came from the U.S. Steelworkers

Union to establish the Players Association and win free agency for the players in the early Seventies. If it weren't for him, these guys would be making peanuts compared to what they're now paid. It's too bad that the Players Association doesn't look at retired players like myself as a part of baseball.

Most of today's younger players don't know much about the game's history. They don't know that players from my era went on strike to give players rights that they still enjoy today. They don't understand that they're making millions of dollars because of us. I'm not saying they owe us anything but a little respect. One exception that I've encountered is Jason Giambi; he really knows the game's history. When I sat down with him, he talked to me about being a designated hitter and was interested in my past. But if you ask many of today's players if they have ever heard of Rod Carew or Jim Palmer, they say, "I think so."

It's a shame, too, as there are some great players who are deserving of enshrinement in the Hall of Fame who haven't made it in, yet. For obvious reasons, Pete Rose isn't in the Hall. But he deserves to be because of what he did on the field—not off it. He was a different type of human being, but I always looked at him favorably for what he has done for the game of baseball. He will always be Charlie Hustle to me.

Goose Gossage and Bert Blyleven should both be in the Hall—absolutely. If Don Sutton could get in—and he deserved to—then you have to vote in Blyleven and Gossage. Unfortunately, enshrinement into the Hall of Fame has become a popularity contest. Dale Murphy might have made it, but he didn't have that New York-Boston-Los Angeles connection that's crucial with the voters in large cities.

As for me, I'm just glad my *bat* is in the Hall of Fame. It's the only bat that's there because of a base on balls, but it's still in Cooperstown. It's also probably the only bat there that has the Star of David scrawled into the knob. One at-bat changed the game—and my life—forever. Some say the designated hitter rule screwed up the game, but I'd rather be associated with a controversial rule than be forgotten.

I want people to think of me not only as someone who was a good athlete, but as someone who is a good person. I loved reaching out to the fans, eating out with my teammates, and hanging out with the writers. I appreciate the recognition I received for my performance on the field, but there's something else that I appreciate more: When talking about me on the radio, John Sterling and Michael Kay would often say, "Ron Blomberg is one of the best guys ever in the game of baseball." I couldn't ask for a greater legacy than that.

EPILOGUE
THE RON BLOMBERG I KNOW

The story of Ron Blomberg would not be complete without including comments from some of the people who knew him best: his son, Adam, daughter, Chesley, first wife, Mara, and longtime agent and friend, Sheldon Stone. Their observations follow.

From Sheldon Stone:

THE NEW MICKEY

"Ronnie came in with big hype. One time he was on the field with Mickey Mantle, and his parents were there. It almost seemed like Mickey was handing the baton to Ronnie to take over. But Ron got a label early: he couldn't hit lefties, so he became a platoon player. And there was criticism about his defense. The Yankees were trying to nurture Bobby Murcer at that time. Ronnie felt they were devoting far more interest and time in Bobby than they were in him."

DEVOTED PARENTS

"Ronnie's parents were very much involved in his life. They lost their other son, so he was an only child at that point. He was the focal point of their lives. The first time I went to their house, the house Ronnie grew up in, I saw pictures of Ronnie in every room. In the center of the basement was a huge, lifesize, cardboard cutout of Ronnie in a basketball uniform. The garage, on the same level of the basement, had a strike zone that had been drawn on it years earlier. The garage had been repainted but they left the strike zone as a Cooperstown-type shrine to Ronnie.

"The one time my wife and I stayed there, we went to bed about 11 o'clock. An hour later, I heard a ballgame. This was Thanksgiving weekend so there were no baseball games. I got up to take a look and found Ronnie's father in the kitchen, listening to a game. I asked him about it. He said he taped a lot of the games and liked to listen to the ones where Ronnie did well. He would relive those games. And he was rooting for Ronnie— *even though he knew what was going to happen.* That's how strongly they were involved with him."

TUESDAYS WITH RONNIE

"When Ronnie first came up, he and his parents became friendly with Elston Howard, who had just retired and was then one of the coaches. Once a week, they would give Elston a call to find out what was going on with Ronnie. They wanted the inside scoop. Once I came into the picture, I inherited the job— much to Elston's delight. Ron never knew about it. His parents would call every Tuesday at 11, even in the off-season, and speak for an hour about what was happening with Ronnie—personally, professionally, and in business. They thrived on that information. No one knew the Blombergs were making these calls. They would ask very detailed questions, and Ron didn't have the patience for that. I felt a lot of compassion for them. I put myself in their shoes and could understand why they called. I didn't tell Ron about it until years later."

MYSTERY GUESTS

"When Ron first came up to New York, he lacked a great deal of sophistication and savvy. In the '70s, there were telethons for the United Jewish Appeal and other Jewish causes. The organizers would try to have appearances by Jewish entertainers and athletes. We did a couple of them from the old Ed Sullivan Theater in New York.

"Before one telethon, they had us wait in the Green Room. The first face I saw when I walked in was Zero Mostel's. Then I recognized Jerry Stiller, Hal Linden, Bette Midler, and a few other very famous people. Ronnie was looking around but didn't look happy. 'They told us we were going to be treated well,' he said, 'and that we were going to be waiting with all the big personalities. Instead, they put us here.' I said, 'What are you talking about? These are the biggest names in show business. Don't you know anybody here?'

"All of a sudden, he said, 'Oh, yeah, you're right. Hey, Soupy!' He recognized Soupy Sales—that's the one person he knew. All the other big names meant nothing to him. He just lacked the city sophistication which, of course, he gained through the years."

COUSIN RONNIE

"I handled all of Ron's appearances. I got a call from a Jewish man who wanted Ron to attend his son's bar mitzvah as a member of the family. I called Ron and told him about it, but he wouldn't do it. When I told him it might be interesting, he said he would go if he got more than his usual fee and if I went with him. I called the man back and he agreed. I asked what he wanted us to do. He said he wanted us there at the conclusion of the service so we could distribute Yankee souvenirs and memorabilia to the kids. He put us in the corridor between the chapel and the reception. The service ended and someone said, 'Look who's here! Cousin Ron Blomberg from the Yankees!'

"The friends of the bar mitzvah boy were coming out of the chapel wearing Yankee helmets. Ron started giving them the paraphernalia. Then we sat at the table with the boy's parents and grandparents. Ronnie had to put a flag in the bar mitzvah cake and give a little speech. We thought we were through, but as we tried to slip out, they played "Take Me out to the Ballgame," the lights came on, and they gave us a standing ovation."

RONNIE'S JEWISH APPEAL

"Jewish fans, especially the ones with some affluence and some time on their hands, all wanted a part of Ronnie. The first time I went into Ron's apartment, he had a big stereo system, carpeting, and furniture. But he hadn't paid for anything—everything was a gift from some store, manufacturer, or Jewish businessman.

"A businessman once called me. He wanted Ron to have dinner with him and his wife at Mamma Leone's. He was offering Ron $3,000 just to do it. Ron refused, but that was the kind of stuff that went on. People would absolutely melt in his presence."

AN ASSIST FROM CATFISH

"When Catfish Hunter came to the Yankees, I asked Ron whether he could get Catfish to make a guest appearance at our baseball camp. He said he would do anything for Ronnie, on one condition: he asked for transportation. But he would not take money from a teammate who was also a friend. When we announced Catfish was coming, a ton of reporters came. It produced tremendous publicity for the camp. Catfish was a sweetheart; he stayed as long as we wanted and would not take any money. There was no snobbery and he had no chip on his shoulder. He treated my secretary as an equal. One time she called him but couldn't reach him. His wife told her he was out hunting dinner."

From Adam Blomberg:

DYNAMITE DAD

"Everybody has a father. And everybody thinks their father is wonderful—he's the man they grew up with. But people know my father as an athlete. When people talk about my dad, they talk about the baseball star. But nobody asks about my father. He's a wonderful father, the most caring person you'll ever meet. I don't know him as a baseball star—I just know him as my father. He is a wonderful, caring individual. He has a heart of gold and would do anything for me, and the rest of our extended family. The one thing I can say about him is that he's a father to be proud of."

LIKE FATHER, LIKE SON?

"Growing up, I was going to be a baseball player. I was a good player, but I wasn't the best. I made all the All-Star teams and the coaches knew who I was. But then, as I started to get out of middle school, the comparisons started to hit. I was going to save my high school team, be a first-round draft pick, and all that. I was lucky I did well in school, because I didn't grow to be six-foot-three and 220 pounds. I was six feet tall and 180. I wasn't going to make the major leagues, and I didn't want to sit in the minors making $10 a day meal money for the rest of my life. So that's why I went down a different path. Rather than playing and listening to the comparisons, I went my own way."

A YANKEE IN BEANTOWN

"Even though I live in Boston now, I'm definitely a Yankee fan. It's a treat to be living in enemy territory. I'm proud of my roots. Most of the attending physicians in my program remember my father. They show respect—even when I walk around wearing a Yankee hat or Yankee jacket. I dress that way out of respect for my father."

From Chesley Blomberg:
AVID YANKEE FAN

"I love everything Yankees. I try to get as much Yankee stuff as I can. I have my dad's baseball cards posted in my room.

Whenever I see people on campus with Yankee caps on, I always say, 'Nice hat.' I haven't met Derek Jeter or Alex Rodriguez yet but I hope to see them every time I go to Old Timers Day at Yankee Stadium with my dad. I love meeting his old teammates and listening to him talk about what the game used to be like and comparing it to what it's like today."

From Mara (Blomberg) Young:

GRANDPA'S APPROVAL

"The morning after I met Ron, I called my grandfather, who was a big Yankee fan. I asked him if he knew the name Ron Blomberg. He corroborated Ron's story and told me how Ron had been the team's top draft choice and was supposed to be a big star. We met on Friday the Thirteenth—June 13, 1969. Three months later, I spent Rosh Hashanah in Atlanta with Ron and his parents."

FAR FROM THE FARM

"I was this Jewish girl from a little city upstate, quite bright but almost like a farm girl. If somebody did something off-color, I'd say, 'This isn't right.' Ron was very similar. I think a lot of the fame, glory, and glitz went right over our heads."

THE REAL RONNIE

"People compared Ron to Mickey Mantle. But he wasn't a switch-hitter, his injuries were different, and he had a different personality. They called him Lil' Abner because of the way he spoke and his knack for saying funny things. But he was bright, quiet, and extremely shy. He was the kind of entertainer who turned into a different person when he put that uniform on. At home, he was the real Ronnie. The personal Ronnie could sit in a room with his legs crossed, watching and observing without talking. The baseball Ronnie could talk your ear off. He was always very kind-hearted. His heart was too big for his body. His father once said to me, 'There will never be another Ronnie in this world.'"

LIFE ON THE DL

"When Ron was injured, he would get up in the morning, read the newspapers, and study the teams and stats. Then he would go to the grocery store, walk around the neighborhood, or do whatever rehab he had to do at the stadium. At night, we would walk for miles around Riverdale. That was the way he got his energy out so he could sleep. He was upset, sad, and concerned for the people who thought he had let them down. He always said, 'I have a life to live, and I'm not going to ruin my body and not be able to live my life when I'm finished. I'm going to get the rehab done properly and go back at the right time.'"

JUST ONE OF THE GIRLS

"I always knew I was the Jewish girl. When I was with the players' wives, I made friends and was friendly. But I knew they knew I was the Jewish wife. I remember sitting in the wives' section one night when someone came up and asked another wife to point me out because they wanted to see what I looked like. The wife said, 'I don't think I'm going to do that.'"

MATCH MADE IN HEAVEN

"I always felt New York City and Ronnie were a perfect fit because of their personalities. He was the perfect vehicle for the Yankees, to have this huge Jewish population and bring them into the ballpark. He never played on Rosh Hashanah or Yom Kippur; a father could look at his children and say, 'Here's this Southern, innocent, fun-loving type of guy and he's one of ours.' We knew New York City liked that because we were very well-received. I loved our life and appreciated it, and Ronnie did, too."

APPENDIX

Ron Blomberg by the Numbers

Bats: Left • Throws: Right • Height: 6'1" • Playing weight: 205 lb.

Year	Team	G	AB	R	H	2B	3B	HR	RBI	BB	SO	BA	OBP	SLG
1969	NYY	4	6	0	3	0	0	0	0	1	0	.500	.571	.500
1971	NYY	64	199	30	64	6	2	7	31	14	23	.322	.363	.477
1972	NYY	107	299	36	80	22	1	14	49	38	26	.268	.355	.488
1973	NYY	100	301	45	99	13	1	12	57	34	25	.329	.395	.498
1974	NYY	90	264	39	82	11	2	10	48	29	33	.311	.375	.481
1975	NYY	34	106	18	27	8	2	4	17	13	10	.255	.336	.481
1976	NYY	1	2	0	0	0	0	0	0	0	0	.000	.000	.000
1978	CHW	61	156	16	36	7	0	5	22	11	17	.231	.280	.372
8 Seasons		**461**	**1,333**	**184**	**391**	**67**	**8**	**52**	**224**	**140**	**134**	**.293**	**.360**	**.473**

Home Run Log

#	Date	Opposing Pitcher/Team	Site
1	6/25/71	Pete Broberg/WAS	NYY
2	7/16/71	Marty Pattin/MIL	NYY
3	8/1/71	Steve Luebber/MIN	MIN
4	8/1/71	Ray Corbin/MIN	MIN
5	8/28/71	Mike Hedlund/KCR	KCR
6	8/28/71	Mike Hedlund/KCR	KCR
7	8/29/71	Dick Drago/KCR	KCR
8	5/7/72	Denny McLain/OAK	OAK
9	5/12/72	Mel Queen/CAL	CAL
10	6/4/72	Tom Bradley/CHW	CHW
11	6/29/72	Jim Palmer/BAL	NYY
12	7/2/72	Milt Wilcox/CLE	NYY
13	7/18/72	Ray Corbin/MIN	NYY
14	7/19/72	Jim Perry/MIN	NYY
15	7/21/72	Lloyd Allen/CAL	NYY
16	7/22/72	Nolan Ryan/CAL	NYY
17	8/13/72	Jim Colborn/MIL	NYY
18	8/19/72	Pete Broberg/TEX	TEX
19	9/19/72	Bill Parsons/MIL	MIL
20	9/23/72	Steve Dunning/CLE	CLE
21	10/1/72	Steve Dunning/CLE	NYY
22	5/8/73	Dick Woodson/MIN	MIN
23	5/13/73	Orlando Pena/BAL	NYY
24	5/18/73	Bill Champion/MIL	NYY
25	7/1/73	Mike Kekich/CLE	NYY
26	7/3/73	Marty Pattin/BOS	NYY
27	7/11/73	Steve Stone/CHW	CHW

#	Date	Opposing Pitcher/Team	Site
28	7/17/73	Dick Woodson/MIN	NYY
29	8/10/73	Horacio Pina/OAK	NYY
30	9/10/73	Dick Tidrow/CLE	NYY
31	9/16/73	Doyle Alexander/BAL	BAL
32	9/23/73	Dick Tidrow/CLE	CLE
33	9/23/73	Dick Tidrow/CLE	CLE
34	4/14/74	Bob Johnson/CLE	CLE
35	4/28/74	Steve Dunning/TEX	NYY
36	4/28/74	Fergie Jenkins/TEX	NYY
37	5/1/74	Catfish Hunter/OAK	NYY
38	6/2/74	Bill Butler/MIN	MIN
39	7/1/74	Joe Coleman/DET	DET
40	9/28/74	Gaylord Perry/CLE	CLE
41	9/28/74	Gaylord Perry/CLE	CLE
42	9/28/74	Tom Buskey/CLE	CLE
43	10/2/74	Jim Colborn/MIL	MIL
44	4/18/75	Joe Coleman/DET	DET
45	4/20/75	Vern Ruhle/DET	DET
46	4/26/75	Bill Castro/MIL	NYY
47	7/8/75	Steve Hargan/TEX	NYY
48	4/7/78	Dick Drago/BOS	CHW
49	4/11/78	Jesse Jefferson/TOR	CHW
50	4/28/78	Dennis Martinez/BAL	CHW
51	6/15/78	Doc Medich/TEX	CHW
52	9/19/78	Alan Wirth/OAK	OAK

ACKNOWLEDGMENTS

This book could not have been completed without the watchful eye of Marty Appel, a longtime New York sports publicist whose tenure as PR director of the Yankees coincided with Ron Blomberg's appearance as the first DH. Marty provided more saves in reviewing this manuscript than Ron's roommate Sparky Lyle did for the ballclub.

Special thanks also go to David Vincent, the affable home-run guru of the Society for American Baseball Research (SABR), for providing valuable research assistance and the home run log that appears in the appendix. His friendship, like Marty Appel's, is highly valued.

So is the relationship with Jeff Idelson, Bill Burdick, and the staff of the Baseball Hall of Fame, who have graciously donated photos for use in this book.

Veteran literary agent Rob Wilson, who knows a good story when he sees one, convinced Sports Publishing that Blomberg's story would not only appeal to baseball historians but also to Yankee fans and a national Jewish audience. A special thanks goes to acquisitions editor Bob Snodgrass and developmental editor Doug Hoepker, who worked with me on previous Sports Publishing projects involving the Florida Marlins and Milo Hamilton. Both of them smoothed the waters whenever the waves got rough.

The author is also grateful to Beth Blomberg, who relayed multiple e-mail messages; to Mara Young, Ron's first wife; to Sheldon Stone, Ron's longtime friend and agent; and to the authors' friends and family, who put up with long hours of meetings and interviewing.

—Dan Schlossberg